These Three Words

Jess van der Hoech

Editing by Sarah Ogden
Cover design by germancreative

thegapbedfordshire.co.uk

For my daughter

PREFACE

I was inspired to write *These Three Words* when, during the course of my work, I discovered there was a huge increase in young people being referred into services for anxiety. The demand was too great for the services to keep up with and many young people were left unable to access support, or had to be placed on a (sometimes very lengthy) waiting list. I wanted to be able to do something to help young people who are not able to access support, as well as those who are not yet ready to speak out about the feelings they are experiencing. There are many fantastic therapy books available which provide the tools for self-help, and many personal stories have been told, both in print and in blog form, by people who have lived with anxiety. I felt that a story of a young person's battle with anxiety, with the tools to cope described within that story, would be a great way to help young people make sense of how and why to use the techniques. I was unable to find such a book, and so the idea for *These Three Words* was born.

I began writing the story of Luna-Ray when I attended a training course to deliver a therapeutic group-work programme, called 'Just What We Need'. It was while I was on this course that I learned many different techniques which I now use in my work, and enormous thanks is extended to Linda Hoggan and Carmen Kane who developed the programme, and who gave me permission to explicitly use their 'Goal Setting' technique, which Sadie teaches Luna in chapter 24. Following the training course, I was inspired to add more content which focused on meeting different emotional needs. If you want to find out more about this, details can be found at JustWhatWeNeed.co.uk. I would also like to thank Dr. Renée Marks, who was co-author on my previous book - *What a Muddle*. I have used some of some of the characters from that book when Sadie explains a bit about the brain to Luna in chapter ten.

My hope is that on reading *These Three Words*, young people will practice some of the techniques that are included, enabling them to find the coping mechanisms that work best for them. I also hope that young people who want to talk about themselves, but don't yet feel able to, can instead talk about Luna in order to help make sense of their own experience. The book will also be invaluable to parents with a child living with anxiety and could help to open up a line of communication with them. However you came to be reading *These Three Words*, I hope that it gives you an insight and understanding into the world of anxiety, and that you find the techniques Luna learns to use as effective as she does.

CHAPTER 1

It's the early hours of Sunday morning, 2.03am to be exact. I can't sleep. I can't sleep because I'm so excited, thinking about the events of the day – one of the best days of my life.

Let me tell you a bit about myself first. My name is Luna-Ray Jones and I'm fifteen years old. I'm a street dancer and take the lead in a dance troupe called 'Starlight'. Today, we took part in a competition with dance troupes from all over the country. Some of them were totally amazing; I was worried for a while that we wouldn't get placed anywhere in the top three, such was the standard of the competition. All twelve of us in the group were nervous, I could tell, but although everyone was thinking it, nobody was saying it. I didn't let my nerves show; one of us at least had to try and hold it together. We were given our five-minute warning, so we all grouped together in the wing and stood in a circle with our hands in the centre. "We can do this," I told the rest of them. "We've worked really hard and we deserve this. Let's go out there and show them what we've got!"

The lights dimmed as we made our way to our places on stage. The music started. I'd mixed our tunes myself - I'm a bit of a DJ as well and I was proud of what I had created for this magical occasion. My legs were going to jelly but I knew that I just needed to focus and push through it, the troupe were depending on me; I couldn't let them down. I forgot about the crowd. I knew there were some people from school out there watching, people I didn't actually like, people who bullied me. This was my chance to show them that I, Luna-Ray Jones, am someone. When the beat dropped I did my thing. I have some moves no one else in the troupe can do yet, even though I have tried and tried to teach them. I don't really like to boast but I am actually a really talented dancer. There was a part where I had to kind of slide across the stage on my head and finish with an impressive spin - still on my head - then get back onto my feet without using my hands. It's no easy task let me tell you, it takes a lot of core strength (which is why I do so many sit-ups, five hundred a day and then I plank for a good fifteen minutes afterwards).

The routine went just as it should have, no mistakes, and as we stood in our finishing positions everyone was smiling and the crowd was going wild. Everyone was clapping and cheering and, well, I don't even know how this happened or who started it but literally everyone was on their feet, chanting my name. "Luna-Ray! Luna-Ray! Luna-Ray!" I felt so happy I could have cried, in fact I probably did. It was so surreal it feels like a bit of a blur. We went back to the wings and the other acts were looking really worried; I could tell by their facial expressions that they were all thinking "How are we going to follow that?"

When the last act had finished, we waited for the results

to come in. Third and second place were announced, it wasn't us and I was really concerned. Had we been disqualified? Maybe our routine was so out of the box and like nothing seen before that we had broken some kind of rule that we didn't know about. Then we heard it. "The winner of the National Street Dancing Championships 2018 is........ (dramatic pause) STARLIGHT!"

Everyone screamed and they were all slapping me on the back and shouting "We did it! It's all thanks to you Luna!" We went on stage once more, this time to collect our prize. Everyone insisted on me going up to the front and collecting the biggest trophy we had ever seen. I lifted it above my head and once again, everyone went wild! Clapping, cheering, foot stamping – it was insane! I could see the girls from my school looking at me open-mouthed from the front row of the balcony. Now they want to know me! Now they know I'm a talented street dancer, that is, who happens to belong to a troupe with some of the fittest lads on the planet in it, who were currently hugging me, lifting me up and spinning me around. The head judge made a speech and said that all three judges had agreed it was one of the most innovative and slickest track mash-ups they had ever heard and the choreography was second to none. I'd initially been given the task of choreographing a small part of the routine but when the rest of the troupe and our coach saw how good I was, they all agreed that I should just do the whole thing. So, yeah, the performance, music, routine and win were pretty much down to me.

I am so happy! I lie on my bed and replay the events once more, the routine music pumping into my ears through my headphones. My cheeks are hurting, I am smiling so much.

The track finishes and I come back to reality. I want to cry. I want to cry because most of what I've just told you is not true.

I can plank for about eighteen seconds and my current sit-up record is approximately four. I've never been near a DJ deck or mixed a track – I wouldn't know how to. There is no dance troupe called Starlight, and even if there was I'm 100% sure my awkward self wouldn't be in it, let alone be the reason behind a national competition win. There is a group of girls at my school who don't bully me, they just make me feel like crap, although I think this is possibly unintentional on their part. They are my friends, I think. Sometimes. Maybe.

The actual real definite truth is this: My name is Luna-Ray Jones, I am fifteen years old and this is the fourth consecutive weekend that I haven't actually left the house. The reason is because I have this condition. When people hear it, they don't get it. They don't realise it's an actual thing that causes really big problems. They don't realise that this condition is ruining my life. I don't think there is a cure for it; I'm likely to be stuck in this horrible cycle for the rest of my entire existence. My name is Luna-Ray Jones, I'm fifteen years old and I have anxiety.

CHAPTER 2

I can't remember exactly when it started. I do remember going to the doctor a few times with a constant sick feeling and stomach pains. I had a load of tests done and they found absolutely nothing. I ended up being diagnosed with Irritable Bowel Syndrome, most likely linked to anxiety. Mum changed my diet and it sort of helped. I thought I had been cured, but then it seemed to come back, slipping into my life unnoticed by everyone, including me at first, until - Bang! There it was, controlling everything again.

I didn't tell Mum when it had come back, I didn't see the point and I didn't want to worry her. There wasn't a big tragedy or a big event or a big anything really. Sometimes I think if there had been, at least people would be able to say "Poor Luna. She was such a lovely outgoing girl until she was involved in that terrible earthquake. She's never been the same since." Without such a tragedy, I can't explain it, and because I can't explain it, I feel really embarrassed about it. If a mate asks me to go somewhere, I don't think I can, so I politely decline, and they stare at me with a confused look and ask "Why don't you want to come shopping? It will be fun." Shopping might be fun for most people, but to me, the thought of walking around a shopping centre, surrounded by strangers and noise with a constant sick feeling in my stomach and a worry that something bad is bound to happen, is not an appealing option. So I won't go.

Sometimes I make up excuses, pretend that I actually have a life and "I'm really sorry but I can't come because I'm already going somewhere very important that day." This tactic can backfire on me when I return to school on the Monday after having politely declined whatever event or occasion it was and I am asked "so, how did it go on Saturday?" By this point I don't have a clue where I was supposed to have been on Saturday because it wasn't actually me that had made the excuse. Anxiety had made the excuse for me and now it is anxiety refusing to provide me with the answer. So anxiety is back in control once again. I look at whoever is asking with a really vacant expression on my face while I desperately plead with anxiety to just go somewhere, anywhere, for just a few seconds so I can get through this interaction, and come out the other side relatively unharmed. But of course anxiety is not a force to be reckoned with, there it is laughing in my face – which by now is probably a deep shade of crimson – my palms are sweating, the washing machine is performing a spin cycle in my stomach and I beg. I beg to be released from this moment, for the ground to open up and swallow me whole, to release me into a land of fairies and wizards and other mythical beings that have no interest in what I did at the weekend, and can make this all just go away. But that doesn't happen. I'm here, in this reality, looking into the face of my friend who is waiting for an answer. What makes it worse is that I absolutely know already that this is not a genuine question, there is no real desire to know how 'it' went on Saturday, she is merely trying to catch me out, to prove that I lied, because she already knows I didn't go anywhere on Saturday. I take the remaining three words my body has to offer and spit them out as fast as I can before I puke. Of course, because of the circumstances, I do not respond like a normal person answering a question. Oh no! Anxiety makes sure that doesn't happen. What actually happens is that the three words are projected with such force that I practically scream in the face of my friend "It got cancelled!" before I turn and run. It probably goes without saying that while all of this is happening internally, externally my body is also responding so even running away becomes awkward and clumsy. My jelly legs seem to be unwilling to carry the weight of the rest of me.

This may all happen within the first five minutes of my entering the school and I am most likely to spend the rest of the day going over and over this exchange in my head. Worrying about it, wondering why I didn't just go shopping, worrying about going shopping, wondering if next time I could just refuse to go shopping, worrying about refusing to go shopping, worrying about who saw and who heard the exchange between me and my friend and then worrying and wondering a bit more about who she has told and who else might be laughing at me.

This happened a few times before I just didn't get invited any more. I can't be sure if I don't get invited because they know I will say no, or because by now they have just decided I am a total weirdo and they don't want to be seen with me anyway.

The group I was friends with – Poppy, Tara and Amy – were never actually horrible or nasty to me in any way. They asked me some awkward questions sometimes, which I didn't answer, but what inevitably happened was this — they carried on being friends, going out and 'developing normally' while I got left behind. We never fell out; it was just that it took more effort to be my friend because there was a lot they couldn't talk to me about. I couldn't talk about going shopping on Saturday or to the cinema on Sunday because I was never there. Having a simple conversation about it became a chore because they would have to explain everything to me first, and they couldn't always be bothered to. Or they would start explaining and then say "oh never mind, it wasn't that funny, guess you had to be there." Every time I heard that, it reminded me that they were normal and I wasn't.

I used to go out. I used to go to places with my family; my family being my mum and my older brother Marley. Marley is eighteen and we get on for about twenty minutes a year, and that twenty minutes is usually made up of two lots of ten minutes at each end of the year. I don't see my Dad; it's always just been Mum, Marley and me. I have Grandparents and Mum's sister Auntie Alice, but they live down South and we don't see them either. I get Christmas and birthday cards from Nan and Grandad and that's about it. We have lived in the Midlands since before I was a year old. I don't know exactly when we moved here, it's not something we talk about much.

When we moved here, I went to nursery while mum worked. It was at Nursery that I met Gigi, who was to become my best friend in the whole world. We went to the same primary school and we were going to go to the same secondary school but that didn't happen, owing to Gigi and her family moving to the other side of the world. Well, they moved to Scotland which is far enough away to validate it being considered the other side of the world, in my opinion. Gigi knows I have anxiety; I told her when she moved away. She's the only one of my friends I've told and she's really supportive about it. She has been back a couple of times to spend a week here in my house. Apart from that, the majority of our best-friendship is now conducted through messages and video chat.

I digress. You know, sometimes I think digression is actually a coping mechanism for anxiety. Without the ability to smoothly divert attention elsewhere in order to entirely avoid something, life becomes a big mass of 'I don't know's. When you're a teenager you're surrounded by people who expect an answer to any question they ask you. Like parents, and especially teachers. Of course they ask questions I can answer like "Why didn't you do your homework?" to which I might say "I didn't understand it, Sir," and Sir might ask: "Why didn't you tell me in the lesson you didn't understand it?" Now at this point I might be thinking: "Well, because I was sitting there feeling sick, and stupid, and hot with shame because everyone else understood it except me, and I didn't want to stand out. Or throw up all over your smart suit as soon as I opened my mouth." But I can't say that because anxiety has decided I only have three words in such a situation, so I use the three words I have come to know best and I simply reply "I don't know."

So when I am asked questions about my anxiety – "When did it start?" and "Why did it start?" – I'm not just trying to avoid the question. I can only tell the truth, and the truth is, I don't know.

CHAPTER 3

I'm struggling to do my school work; it's really hard. I don't understand most of it, and the bits I do understand I'm really behind on. This is what happens sometimes. As a class we get set a piece of work. We can make a start on it during the lesson and then we are supposed to do the rest as homework. If I don't understand it, I generally create an action plan for how I am going to do the work. I do a brainstorm, for example, but there are no ideas or any actual words written on the diagram, it is just a very beautiful outline. I will colour it in, write my name in beautiful letters at the top of the page, decorate it all and manage to spend the whole remainder of the lesson doing nothing productive, while looking like I am indeed very busy. I usually don't understand what I am supposed to be doing or the task that was set.

So then of course, I have to finish it off at home. I remove the beautiful outline of what was supposed to be some sort of diagram from my bag and I feel like a failure because I haven't done any work. Then I look at the work and somehow – and I'm not even sure how this happens – I seem to know even less about what it is I'm supposed to be doing, so I put it away. When the time comes for the work to be handed in, I don't have any work to be handed in and I can sometimes be berated by the teacher in front of the class. This makes me hate the teacher and dislike the subject further.

Sometimes I *do* understand the work. Great! So I get on with it, without the need for beautiful diagrams or brainstorming of any sort. I write the whole thing out, and before I hand it in, I check it. This may be in plenty of time; I might have a week to go if I have finished the work on night one. So I decide that as I have six more days to complete this piece of genius, I can do a bit better, and I start it again. I decide eventually that the work I have produced is not good enough. No one has seen it apart from me, nor will they ever see it because it is likely to embarrass me. I throw it away and start again. Then the night before it is due in, I write something in a panic that is nothing like the standard of what I produced on night one, and I either don't hand it in, or I hand it in and get a low grade.

Both of these scenarios leave me feeling deflated. There are no other scenarios, just these; I'm in a constant cycle of trying and failing or failing to try. I don't think I fail to try myself, but that is what I hear quite a bit from my teachers. They will say something really supportive and encouraging like "You're a very bright girl; I know you can do better." But what I hear is "You're not good enough."

I think as a result of my age, my lack of desire to do anything in the future and the constant criticism I receive, I have begun to hate school. I think maybe that's why the anxiety started; the humiliation... the constant humiliation.

Sometimes, teachers are going around the room, picking on people to answer a question. They get to me and I can't get the words out in the right order. I know I won't be able to string a sentence together. I cannot face suffering this kind of humiliation, which is why they receive a three worded answer – "I don't know."

The ultimate result is this: I *hate* school.

I've made another half-hearted attempt at a history project about 'Bloody Sunday', but I still don't get it. I decide that actually now would be a good time to call Gigi. When I fail to hand some work in at school tomorrow, I will at least be safe in the knowledge that my time was spent doing something much more fun.

I video-call with Gigi quite often. She has always been and will always be my very best friend. I know I have mentioned this before, but the reason I like mentioning it, is because I enjoy hearing myself say it. I enjoy knowing I have a best friend. I don't talk to many other people really, I'm not sure I actually like people if I'm brutally honest, but I like Gigi very much.

She picks up on the third ring. "Hey beautiful," she says as she answers. This is another reason I like Gigi so much. She says things like this quite a lot of the time and even though I don't believe that I'm beautiful, it's nice to hear it, especially from someone who isn't my mum.

"Hey yourself," I tell her, as I am now forbidden from addressing her as 'beautiful' because that would be copying. She is very beautiful though. She has blonde curls and bright blue eyes and skin like a porcelain doll. The total opposite of me, with my mousey brown, straight hair and crooked tooth.

Unlike me, Gigi *is* beautiful and she also seems happy to know this to be true.

"What you up to?" It would be lovely to have an exciting story to tell her, to be able to say I've been somewhere or done something or seen someone, but I haven't.

"Nothing."

"What, nothing nothing or just nothing?"

"Nothing nothing."

"Have you been out this weekend?"

"No," I tell her, because this is the truth. She looked like she was about to say something but then stopped herself before she did.

"What were you going to say?" I ask her, now desperate to know her answer.

"Nothing."

"Don't lie to me, Gigi, I know your face, what were you going to say?"

"Well, I was just going to point out the obvious, that you haven't done anything at the weekend for a while now, not even gone out with your mum." Two things surprised me. One was that she had noticed and the other was that she was saying something to me about it.

"Rub it in, why don't you?"

"No, Luna don't be like that! I was only saying!"

Worried that an argument was looming, I needed to change the subject. Gigi was my constant; I couldn't fall out with her. I have the ability to fall out with people quite quickly; especially Mum. I don't even understand where the anger I have comes from sometimes, one minute I'll feel fine and the next I'm in a rage and it can be really hard to control. I wanted to tell Gigi that I have this fear right now, that something 'big' is about to happen. I don't even know what, it's like there's something in the air. I feel like I'm getting worse. The switch is being flicked on and off inside me, one minute I think I'm alright, the next I feel like I'm out of control. It's never been like this before, but without being able to explain it, it's going to be a difficult conversation to have, even with Gigi and I think we might be on the verge of a fall-out.

I guess I was quite relieved when she said "'Anyway, it's not important, what have you been doing?" Gigi knew when to leave something with me, she didn't go on and on about it, plus I knew she had started seeing some boy and she would be desperate to talk about him. "Jay came over on Friday night, we hung out for a while, went out to get some chips, sat at the park and ate them. It was good, it was chilled."

"Did you eat them in front of him?"

"No Luna, I went and sat in a bush and ate them! Of course I ate them in front of him!"

I don't know how she could do that. If she really liked him, why would she eat in front of him? I could never do such a thing. If I liked a boy, I'm not sure how I would feel about him knowing that I ate, never mind doing it in his presence.

"What else did you do?"

"Not a lot really."

Gigi then went on to tell me in great detail about kissing him for pretty much most of the night. I feel too awkward to repeat this conversation and I wouldn't want to betray her trust, even though she pretty much ended the call with me because he popped up on her laptop and she had to go and talk to him.

This is the biggest difference between me and Gigi. She has this confidence about her that I could only ever dream of having. She does amazing things like going out and eating chips with her boyfriend. I want to speak highly of Gigi all the time. I want to be able to talk about all the great qualities she has, but tonight I don't feel like I can for two reasons. The first is that what she had just said rattled me. She basically annoyed me and then dropped me to go and talk to her boyfriend. I don't want to say that I feel jealous because I'm not. I want to be happy for her but I don't really have a place in her life anymore; she's just another person moving on without me. I think that maybe she has just deliberately pissed me off so it would be easier to drop me; that way she can blame me and say it's because I wasn't being very entertaining or I'm in a mood. It's probably best that she did hang the phone up because I wouldn't have wanted her to be on the receiving end of my rage.

I didn't used to be a 'ragey' kind of girl, but just lately, I keep getting these overwhelming surges of anger. I project three words with such venom and I don't even feel like I can control it anymore. The words are out there before I can take them back. Then I feel upset because I've just lost control and hurt someone else. Usually Mum or Marley, which is fine because they just put up with me, but I can feel this anger starting to boil over where I really don't want it to, like school. People aren't as easily forgiving at school. You do one thing and seven months later people are still banging on about it like it was a recent thing. This hasn't actually happened to me personally, but it has happened to other people. Ruth Edwards in the year above me supposedly got drunk at the park, puked and declared her undying love for

Mr. Hartley who teaches computer studies. I didn't even know who Ruth Edwards was until I heard that story. This was the version that people were talking about in the corridors, in the canteen, everywhere. Tara's sister is friends with her and she said that what *actually* happened was that someone spiked Ruth's coke with the vodka they were drinking and Ruth spat it out and went home because she didn't want to be around the drunk people she happened to be friends with. She said she was going home to do her computer studies homework which was where Mr Hartley came into it. So, even the slightest little event can get turned into something massive. If I raged at school in the morning by lunchtime the story would probably be that I'd murdered someone.

I hate this. I hate not being in control and I hate feeling so angry with Gigi. I really want to be happy for her; if I was a true friend, I would be happy for her, not sitting here nearly crying because she said goodbye to me to talk to someone else. I felt guilty because I already knew if I called Gigi back, she would talk to me. She wouldn't hold it against me that I'd been a bit of an arse with her, she just seems to get that I don't always see things the same way other people see them, and that's the end of it.

It got me thinking that perhaps the only way I am going to keep the friends I have is to keep up with them. Maybe I should start going out with someone so we would have something in common once again. At least then we would be able to share our stories of what we had been doing with our boyfriends and I would once again feel accepted – normal, even. But I couldn't ever see myself going out with anyone. If someone told me that so-and-so fancied me, I'd automatically think it was a joke. I'd think I was being set up to admit that I really liked him just for him to turn around and say "What, you thought that was serious?" and then everyone would find out and laugh at me.

Even if it did so happen that one day I met a boy and he liked me and I liked him and we got together, I don't think I'd be able to kiss him. Because what would happen if it turned out I was really bad at it and he told everyone? I'd turn out to be Luna-Ray Jones, breath smells of onions, terrible kisser and that would be it for the rest of my life. No marriage, no children, no future. Not worth the risk.

I lie back on my bed. I already know what is going to happen tonight. I will be worried about going to school because I haven't done my school work. The worry about it is so overwhelming it is interfering with my ability to actually produce anything to hand in. So I will worry about not being able to do it, I will worry about not doing it, I will worry about going to school in general and going to school without any work to hand in. I will worry about Gigi and whether or not she still wants to be friends with me because she is officially growing up and Jay is now more important than I am, even though we promised each other that that would never happen. And to top it all off I'm now going to worry about how I'm going to get out of kissing a boyfriend I don't even have.

CHAPTER 4

It is Sunday morning. I slept OK when I eventually nodded off around 2.30am. I assume it must have been around this time as it was 2.27am when I last looked at the clock and clock-checking has become one of my favourite hobbies. Mum woke me up around 9am. I am still really tired as I venture downstairs. As I approach the kitchen Mum starts.

"Well done for getting up Luna, I know you like a lie in at the weekend but you'll regret it if you sleep in too late today, it will make it harder to get up for school tomorrow." She carries on talking but all I can hear is a noise that is similar to "Blah, blah blah, blah blah blah," and so it goes on. In congratulating me for getting up, she has mentioned school which is like firing an air horn at anxiety, which has now also decided it is a good time to wake up.

I *hate* school. The word leads to the thought of it which starts the all too familiar feeling of sickness swishing around my stomach, the hand of anxiety encouraging it, increasing the feeling as the seconds tick on. Up until now, I'd thought I was hungry. I have got as far as opening the fridge and looking inside. There is nothing good jumping out at me, so I shut the fridge door, wait for a second then open it again in case there is good food in there which hasn't been so quick to hide this time. Nothing magically appears and Mum is still going on, and on. And *still* all I can hear is 'Blah blah blah' until she snaps.

"Luna! Are you even listening?"

"What?!" I snap back, my tone matching hers.

"I want you to clean that pigsty of a room up today. You might be willing to take the chance of living with vermin with all that rubbish you have in there, but I'm not! Get it done!"

I look at her. I can feel my eyes narrowing into the death stare. This is her fault. If she hadn't mentioned school, I would have come downstairs, eventually found something delicious to eat and I'd be sitting eating my lovely breakfast and everything would be alright. Instead the worrying has started, the sick feeling is there and I know it won't go away now. My whole day is ruined. I feel so angry, so very angry with her, and I know I have three words I can safely project before I puke. I need to make sure I choose those words carefully. I don't want to have a conversation or a nice chat; I need to get her off my case. So with the force I need to get the words out, I manage to scream "I HATE YOU!" at her before I run back up the stairs to the safety of my room.

My breathing has quickened, a mixture of the run up the stairs and the panic setting in. It feels like a heavy weight on my chest, crushing my lungs. I grab my phone and put my headphones in and quickly flick to a random track on my playlist. It's *The Killers*, 'Mr Brightside'. I love this song. I imagine myself in the band. I am playing guitar. We are on stage at Wembley and no one can play guitar quite like me. I am the reason this band is together. As the track comes to an end, I imagine the crowd screaming my name "Luna-Ray! Luna-Ray! Luna-Ray!" I feel calmer. The sick feeling is still there but the panic is starting to ease off, drifting away just enough to bring me back to reality.

I think back to when I first started to love that song. Mum had been singing it for days, very badly I might add, saying "You must know this song Luna!" but I didn't recognise it. In fairness, *The Killers* probably wouldn't have recognised what song it was from the version her vocal chords were producing. She had put it on and we danced around the room like crazy people. She didn't even tell me off when I started jumping on the sofa. The song deserved some serious jumping and I needed the assistance of the sofa springs to power me up. We danced and jumped around until we were out of breath, collapsing on the sofa in a fit of giggles. I like it when she is being 'fun mum'.

I think back to our encounter in the kitchen which feels like hours ago now, even though it has actually only been a few minutes. This is another trick of anxiety; it can put a completely different perception on time. Mum had looked tired. Marley had been out with his mates the night before and I know Mum had stayed awake to make sure he got home, which was after midnight. I know this to be true because I heard him come in myself. Mum is always up early, says her body is programmed for 5am starts; she doesn't even need an alarm. I wonder, if I went out and stayed out until after midnight, would mum even wait up for me? Probably not. Marley has always been her favourite. I can't give an example of a time when Mum has proven this to be the case, but no matter what Marley does or how rude he is to her; Mum never turns her back on him.

I can hear her on the phone. I think she is talking to Audrey, Gigi's Mum. They are really good friends; they met while Gigi and I were at nursery. I creep to my door so I can listen in to the conversation better.

"....know he's smoking that cannabis......thinks I can't smell it......worried about both of them.......just screamed she hates me.....can't do anything right Aud..."

I back into my room again; I don't want to hear any more. I feel really bad now. I know Mum has a lot on her plate. Marley thinks his ganja smoking is a big secret, but we both know. He's really moody all the time and Mum thinks he's going to end up being kicked out of college. She hadn't meant to upset me before; she hadn't meant to make me feel angry. She doesn't even know I feel the way I do, she just thinks I'm a hormonal teenager. I know this to be the case because I heard her telling Audrey once. I know Gigi won't say anything to her mum, I can trust Gigi. I wish I knew how to explain it to my mum, but I wouldn't know where to start. She would have loads of questions and I would have a lot of 'I don't know' answers. I want to apologise but I'm not ready to face her. It would only end up in an argument anyway and I really don't have the energy to deal with all of that.

I look at my room, remembering her request for me to clean it up. I suppose if I tidied it, it would kind of make it up to her. I'll do that then. Where do I start though? Even though my room is probably messier than the average messy room, I don't really seem to notice it. I like to be able to see all my lovely things around me. To me, my things are all lovely and have real meaning, and such wonderful memories attached to them. I couldn't bear to part with them. I mean, what would happen if I threw something away and it had a wonderful memory attached to it and in throwing it away, the wonderful memory went with it? This is why I keep so much stuff. Oh and because if the truth be known, I'm scared of throwing things away. What if I threw something away and then needed it the next week? What if I threw something away that I was actually supposed to keep? Something disastrous might and probably would happen. So I keep things, lots of things. If I was to be really totally truthful, even I would have to admit that actually, not all of my things are even that lovely. I just have piles of stuff.

I look to my right to my dressing table. It's a pile of pictures and posters that I used to cut out from a pop magazine that I subscribed to when I was going through my 'pop' phase. I'd covered an entire bedroom wall with these posters. Each week, I'd cut the pictures from the magazines, carefully checking both sides of the page to make sure if there was another picture on the other side, that I was selecting the better one for my wall. Big pictures, little pictures, posters, all pictures of my favourite boy band at the time. It was guaranteed that every week their cute little faces would be appearing in the magazine and I would cut them out, ever so carefully, apologising if I accidentally caught one of them in the eye with my scissors, and saved them until I had enough to cover the wall. When Mum said I could stick them all up on the wall, I was so excited that I got to work right away. Mum had said to use Blu-tac but there was no time to look for Blu-tac and why bother when there was sticky tape right there! So taped up they were. They were a little more tricky to get down when I went through my next phase (Emo), and I wanted to replace them with something else. Each picture, no matter how carefully I tried to remove it, ripped at the corners. The tape marked the walls. Mum wasn't very happy about that. So now I am left with a pile of posters and pictures with ripped edges that were removed from my wall about two years ago. I can't bear to throw them away, I mean what if I start to like them again? The band isn't together anymore, so I would never be able to replace this collection. Maybe in twenty years or so, they might be worth something. I'd had this conversation with Mum when I had taken them down and decided to keep them. I think her words were "For God's sake Luna, scrappy pictures from a magazine in mass production will not be of any value either now, or at any time in the future. If you had an entire collection of magazines from the start to the end of their time in print, maybe *that* would be worth something in about a hundred years."

"Really?!" I'd said, my eyes lighting up with the thought of the riches my great, great grandchildren had coming their way. "Brilliant! Because I've still got all the magazines too!" Mum had looked at me with quite a puzzled face.

"Luna-Ray," she said, her tone of voice changing to one she might usually reserve for a three-year-old. "You cut the pictures from the same magazines didn't you?"

"Yes," I confirmed, very slowly, my tone matching hers.

"So the magazines won't be worth anything because they are no longer intact. The pictures won't be worth anything because they have been cut out of the magazines. So what you actually have is a pile of rubbish, which needs to go in the bin."

I felt utterly heartbroken and deflated in that moment, like a balloon that had just had all the air let out of it. I ran back upstairs, bin liner in hand, gathered together all of my precious magazines and posters and put them in the bin liner. I then put the sack in the bottom of the wardrobe. Over time, the pictures have made their way out of the bin liner and are back in their pile, which is now next to my dressing table.

I've make a pact with myself that I will have a clear out, I will get everything together on my bed and attempt to sort through it. I only ever make new piles of stuff and nothing gets thrown away. This same regime has applied to most of my stuff – make-up, clothes that I don't wear anymore, shoes, school stuff – everything really. Logically I know I should have thrown the lot away, but this is what anxiety does. It sends a whole load of 'what if's and 'maybe's around and around my head and the outcome, whichever way I play it, is going to be bad. So even today, while looking round my room and deciding where to start, before I have even picked up and looked at one single object, anxiety has already decided that each and every one of my pointless, worthless collections is going to stay.

CHAPTER 5

I didn't really do much yesterday. After looking around my room, making some new piles and once again keeping everything, I managed to waste another day trying really hard not to think about school. I've managed to avoid school entirely some days, telling Mum I felt sick and she let me stay off. When she started questioning my ongoing sickness, I switched to migraines. I do actually feel sick and get headaches quite a lot so I'm not totally lying. Then school started getting on Mum's case about my attendance so it was easier to start going in again.

I still haven't actually managed to tell her how bad I am feeling inside; I'm certain that she wouldn't understand. Every now and then I spend a lesson or two hiding in the girls' toilets but this isn't ideal either. Today I've been having a particularly bad day, I just have a feeling that something is going to happen but I don't know what, so I'm already on edge. I wander into the lunch hall at 1.38pm. I know this to be the precise time because I just checked my phone.

Phone-checking is another big thing for me. I like to know

it's there and if my phone is in my hand, I feel better than I do without it. Not only does it have the time, it is my lifeline to the outside world that I don't really feel a part of. It's a Smartphone so it has access to the internet, all my social media apps that make me feel connected to something and my beloved music collection – all in this tiny contraption. It is *such* an amazing invention. Who was it that found out that by dialling a small series of numbers, you could be connected to another person anywhere in the world? Not only that, but when you speak to them there's no huge time delay and they sound exactly the same as they do in real life. I don't call anyone except Gigi and sometimes Mum (who doesn't count), because I don't actually like talking on the phone, it's too awkward. But if I wanted to, it's possible, and I think that's genius.

So here I am walking into the dinner hall and Tara catches my eye and half waves at me. I start to make my way over as Tara says something to Poppy and Amy and they all start laughing. I know it's about me and I feel sick. I don't want to go over anymore. They'll feel awkward too because they'll have to stop finding me so hilarious and make something up, so I turn around and walk back out of the canteen. I need to be away from them, away from this feeling. I put my headphones in and walk around for a bit, trying to forget what has just happened. I imagine I am an actress arriving at the premiere to my latest film. The paparazzi are all photographing me and shouting my name "Over here Luna! Come and talk to us!" They all want that exclusive interview with me but my gorgeous bodyguard stands between me and them, protecting me, shielding me from the flashes of the cameras, keeping me safe. I'm untouchable. I like this thought, I'll have it again sometime. Time has flown as I've been wandering, lost in my crazy imagination. I can hear the ring of the school bell faintly behind the music still playing in my ears. I hope maths goes as quickly as the last twenty minutes have.

I have to psyche myself up to walk into the classroom. I've arrived at the same time as everyone else and I try to slip in unnoticed. Tara is already in her seat next to mine and she turns as I walk up to the desk.

"Hey Luna, what happened to you at lunch? I thought you were coming over."

I busy myself looking in my bag trying to ignore the flush I can feel creeping into my cheeks. How could she? They were blatantly taking the piss out of me and now she wants to know why I didn't join in? I rummage in my bag a bit longer. I can see my maths book and my pencil case, which are all I need, but if I take them out, I will have nothing to look in my bag for, nowhere to hide. I have to keep my answers short. "I went library."

Tara seems not to notice anything is wrong and she carries on, "Oh my God, Luna you should have been there! Poppy fancies Luke Bailey, she decided last week he is the one for her, except he doesn't seem to notice she's alive, so in English when he was talking about a dancing dog, Poppy decides to seize the moment and starts saying 'Oh, I'd love to see it, I love dogs!' Honestly Luna, can you imagine it? Poppy who has no interest in animals whatsoever! So anyway, she thinks the dog belongs to Luke, so she's asking to set up a meeting so he can bring his dog to the park or whatever...."

I've stopped looking in my bag because I don't even think Tara would notice if I grew horns, she is so into this elaborate story she's inventing, so I let her carry on.

"….said that he would sort it out later on, so there she is being a bit full of herself when Amy says 'you'd better check your news feed' and he's posted this video on her wall, honestly Luna we were cracking up!" As if to demonstrate her point, Tara dissolves into a fit of giggles once again but then notices that I'm not laughing, or smiling or reacting in any way. I could have predicted her next sentence, the way the majority of conversations finish around me these days.

"Guess you had to be there."

I don't think it could be possible for me to feel any worse than I do in that moment but hearing those words somehow makes that happen, and I want to cry.

Miss Baker walks in at that moment. We have a mutual dislike of one another. Last parents evening she told my mum that I am a day-dreamer who doesn't pay enough attention and I am going to fail maths. I don't understand the subject anyway and the pressure I feel from her is so intense. She could humiliate me in a second and I know she is likely to do just that. I want to get away. As I sit here, the feeling just intensifies, and I can feel myself starting to sweat. My friends are taking the piss out of me, Miss Baker hates me and I've just noticed everyone on my table has a graph in front of them that I now realise is homework that I haven't done. I'd completely forgotten about it. I hadn't accidentally forgotten about it, I'd deliberately forgotten about it because I didn't understand it. Miss Baker has clocked me, sitting in my seat without a graph in front of me and is making her way over. Everyone is watching her so it's inevitable that every pair of eyes will follow her and land on me and I really can't cope with it. Miss Baker has her favourite students and it is a well-known fact that I'm not one of them. My palms are sweating, my cheeks are going red, I need to get out of here but the door is the other side of the classroom. I can feel the panic on its way; it's like standing on a platform of the underground waiting for a train, you can hear it coming in the distance and you think it's far away and then whoooosh! There it is in front of you, waiting for you to get on. Panic sets in like that for me, except unlike the underground, there's no timetable to tell you when it's coming. There's no warning, it's just there.

"Where's your homework?" Miss Baker is standing over me, making me feel much smaller than I actually am. I can't say anything; I'm just trying to remember how to breathe. "Oh don't tell me, you forgot didn't you? Again!"

Someone sniggers behind me. All of a sudden I realise that I'm crying. I see the first tear drop and fall onto my lap. "Luna-Ray you can't start crying every time you fail to do something, you're not nine anymore, grow up!"

Something snaps; it is all too much. I have to go, I have to get away. The rage comes with such force that before I even realise what I am doing, before I realise that I have these three words to project, before I have a chance to think about the consequences of what I am about to do, I scream "JUST FUCK OFF!" in Miss Baker's face and get up from the table. I leave my book and pencil case on the table in front of me and grab my bag only because it has my phone in it. I get up and I run, I just run, I have to get out, I need to be somewhere safe; I need to be at home. I manage to make it out of the front gate of the school, and run down the road, across the green, past the shops and along the main road. I just keep running and I don't stop.

I make it to the top of my street and pause to catch my breath. I don't know what just happened. Even though I'm out of breath from running, my heart is pounding and my head is all fuzzy; I feel better. I'll be okay now; I can see my front door. Walking calmly up to it, I let myself in, get a glass of water from the kitchen and take it upstairs. I put the glass on the side, collapse onto my bed, and cry.

I cry as I remember how my friends laughed at me. I cry as I realise I have just sworn at a teacher and run out of school before the end of the day. I cry even harder when I think about how I am going to explain this to Mum. None of this seems real; I really don't know what is happening to me. I spend a few more minutes crying before I start to calm down. I need a distraction. I log into Facebook and there it is at the top of my newsfeed. Luke Bailey has shared a video on Poppy's wall; a video of a dancing dog. And I start to cry once more.

CHAPTER 6

Mum has just got home and I'm still tearful. I don't know what's happening to me; I'm sure I am getting worse. I have never run from a classroom before and left school. I have never sworn at a teacher. I knew something big was going to happen this morning; I just pray that the worst is over. Mum's home early, I wonder if she knows what I've done?

"Luna!" she calls out, pretty much as soon as she walks through the door. Maybe if I don't answer, she won't know that I'm here. I stay quiet with this hope but I hear her footsteps coming up the stairs.

"Luna.....you're here," she says as she walks into my bedroom. She stands at the door, her hand on her hip. She has a face on her that says 'you're in trouble' before any words leave her mouth.

"Do you want to tell me what the bloody hell you're playing at? I've just had a call from Mr. Davis to tell me that my daughter has thought it appropriate to shout at a teacher before not only running from the class, but leaving the school entirely. Why the bloody hell did you do that?"

She is shouting as she says this, let's not be mistaken about it, she isn't calm and rational and therefore, nor am I. She can have three words:

"I don't know."

"You don't *know*? I have had to leave work early, I have had to explain to my boss that my stupid daughter has potentially gone missing and I need to go and find her. Do you know how embarrassing that is for me?"

Something snaps. I don't know where it came from, I didn't believe I had enough energy for a rage left, but no, I am somehow able to find enough to make this day even worse.

"It's all about you, isn't it Mum? You don't even care about what happened, you haven't even asked me. You just listened to some stupid teacher, who wasn't even there, and you walk in here and start having a go; you haven't even asked me if I'm okay! Well if you want the answer then no, I'm not okay, I'm not okay!" And to prove this point, I punch myself in the face, hard. I'm sitting up on my bed, hot tears streaming down my face, spitting my words out like venom. I could probably see Mum's frightened face if I could see through the tears, but I didn't even feel like this was me.

"I hate my life! I'm ugly," I punch myself in the face, "I'm stupid," another punch, "I'm a total fucking weirdo!" another punch that is stopped by something, and I realise that it's Mum's arm.

She pulls me towards her and holds me tight. I start to fight her off me so I can carry on fighting myself, but I suddenly realise I don't have the energy to carry on. I cry. Big, hot tears are streaming down my face, mixed with lashings of snot, as I wail. I can vaguely sense Mum rocking me, I can't see her; she is behind me with one arm wrapped around my waist, the other stroking my hair.

We stay like that for a good ten minutes as I continue to cry. Eventually the wailing stops, the tears stop and I let out a sigh. Mum takes this opportunity to turn my head round so I am facing her. I turn my whole body round so she can see me. She has been crying too.

"Luna, what on earth has happened?"

"I don't know," I tell her, truthfully. "I don't know what's wrong with me Mum, my life's just a mess and I don't know what to do." I start crying again but more calmly this time.

"Luna, go and splash some cold water on your face and come downstairs so we can have a proper talk. I'll make some tea."

I'm really glad she said that because clearly all I need is a sodding cup of tea. Why didn't I think of that before?

I go into the bathroom and splash myself with warm water, not cold. The shock of cold water would be too painful for my burning face. I return to my room where I change into my comfiest tracksuit bottoms and hooded top before I go and face the music. I don't bother planning what I'm going to say, as there can be no more excuses. I think it's time to tell her the truth.

Mum is sitting at the small table in the kitchen when I go down. She puts a cup of tea in front of me.

"Three sugars. It will help you feel better." I think I probably need more than three sugars and so will she by the time I've finished.

"What's going on Luna? I don't understand."

The tears are going to come again, I can feel them. "I couldn't stay in that room with her Mum."

"Who?"

"Miss Baker."

"Why?"

"I forgot to do my homework and she came over and just started shouting at me in front of everyone. She hates me. I just couldn't stay. I didn't plan on leaving, it just sort of happened." Mum is looking into her cup like it might have an answer at the bottom of it.

"I don't understand, Lu."

"Nor do I, Mum, that's the point! I hate feeling like this but it won't go away."

"Like what?"

"Anxious."

"But I took you for all those tests and the doctor said there was nothing wrong with your stomach. You stopped saying you had stomach aches, I thought you were better now"

"So did I Mum. But it just got worse and worse and I didn't know what to do. I hate being at school, I hate going out, I have no friends, the teachers hate me, people are always talking about me and you just have a go at me all the time."

"No, I don't!"

I stand up. "There you go again, you never listen to me! You're always on about the state of my room that's all you care about. Having a go at me and caring about Marley, even though he is a total arsehole."

"Luna, I don't treat you any differently." I am pacing around the kitchen now; I just need to keep my legs moving.

"You do though Mum, you don't pay me any attention."

"You're always in your room with your headphones in."

"Only because there's nothing else to do!"

"I'm always suggesting you go out with your mates, I've said I'll take you to the cinema or out for something to eat and you always say no."

"Mum, I'm scared of going out. I don't want to be at the cinema; I'd rather stay here and be ignored by you. I hate school, I hate everyone there, no one gets me..." I can't even finish my rant because I'm crying again. My face is starting to feel a bit sore now as well where I hit myself. I sit back down at the table.

"Mum I just feel like I don't want to be here anymore, I can't live like this, it's too much. It's never going to get any better!" Mum openly bursts into tears as she walks over to me and hugs me again. I keep my arms firmly in the pockets in the front of my top.

"Oh Luna, don't ever say that, you're just having a bad day."

"It's not a bad day though, Mum, it's a bad friggin' lifetime! I feel like this every single day. I hate it!"

"How long?"

"How long what?"

"How long have you felt like this?"

"I don't know Mum. Get off me now please." I hate being touched. Especially like that, arms wrapped around me so tight I can hardly breathe and not really move. Mum steps back and looks at me.

"I'm going to take you to the doctor's. We'll go tomorrow and get this sorted."

"OK." I'm quite impressed that she seems to be taking this seriously.

"I'll take the day off work. Oh, bugger!" she runs from the room. "I need to ring Mr Davis and tell him you're alright!" See how quickly her attention can be diverted? One minute it's about me, the next it's Mr Davis.

I feel tired, so tired. I leave the kitchen, my tea untouched, and head to my room, where I lie on my bed for approximately six seconds before falling into a deep sleep.

CHAPTER 7

I'm sitting in the waiting room with Mum, feeling really sick already. Dr. Jackson has been our GP for years but I can't work out if that makes it better or worse. When I come to see him for normal stuff like sore throats and the stomach pains, it's so much easier because it's like I actually have a pain that he can treat. What if he can't do anything for me? What if he just says "I'm very sorry to hear about this, Luna-Ray, but that's it; get used to it and welcome to the rest of your life"? Then again, maybe he has a magic anxiety pill that'll make it all go away. I've been thinking about this and I have decided that this is the way forward. I think this is why Mum has brought me here, because maybe she knows there is a pill I can take that will make everything better. I feel slightly better knowing that in a few minutes I will have a prescription in my hand that will contain the answer to all my problems. I feel a tiny bit better with this thought in my mind, but not enough for the sickness to go away.

Mum is reading a magazine from about twenty years ago that she found on the table in the waiting room and every now and then she tries to distract me with something from it that I have approximately zero interest in. She's starting to annoy me, tapping my leg and in a hushed voice saying "Oh now look at this Luna, doesn't she look stunning?" while showing me a picture of some has-been celebrity in a crap dress.

I really want to tell her to shut up but instead I play a mantra in my head on repeat: *she's only trying to help... she's only trying to help...*

I just want to go home. Mum has already told me I can have the rest of today off of school and I'm looking forward to going back to my lovely warm bed and watching rubbish daytime TV. Maybe we can bypass the doctor totally and just go straight home and I can spend the next three years just comfortably lying in bed? He could post me my prescription instead. I could get a job providing feedback on daytime telly. The producers of these morning shows would ring me up... no they wouldn't, I don't like talking on the phone... they would message me... no email me, because email is for professionals, and they'd ask me questions like "What do you think was missing from the telly this morning, Luna-Ray?" and I would reply and tell them that what I did and didn't like watching. Oh, and I could also send them ideas on what the presenters should be wearing to make them look more appealing. I'd get paid for staying in bed, watching TV and sending emails. I wonder if there is a job like that out there? There should be; if there isn't, maybe they could create it and I could do it. That's the rest of my life sorted! So I don't need to worry about talking to the Doctor.

Just as I'm about to give Mum the good news, Dr. Jackson comes out into the waiting room and calls my name.

Mum stands up to come in too. I don't mind this because she always comes in to the doctor's with me and I usually leave it to her to explain why I'm there. I like Dr. Jackson. He's a kindly looking man, probably in his fifties, with thick-rimmed round glasses and a cheery-looking face. He's a nice man and he's always patient and understanding. I like him.

We walk into his room and sit in front of his desk. The stethoscope and other medical-looking things are on the desk and the pot of stick things that he pushes your tongue down with to check if you have tonsillitis are also there. Ever since I was little, I have believed them to be lollypop sticks and no matter how old I get, I don't think anyone will ever convince me that actually they aren't. "They are professional pieces of medical equipment." Nope, they're lolly sticks.

"What can I do for you, young Luna-Ray?" he asks in his cheery, booming voice.

I look at Mum and get ready for her to answer, but instead of answering so he can give me a magic pill and send me on my way, Mum starts crying. God she's *so* embarrassing!

"She hasn't been herself for months, Doctor. I thought she was just being a teenager and that it was all down to her hormones, but it came out last night that there's something more to it."

Dr. Jackson looks at me with interest. He sits back in his chair and folds his arms across his stomach. This is the pose he always takes when there's a long conversation to be had. I've seen it before.

"Luna-Ray?" he half asks, half says. I stop biting my nails and look at him.

"Mmmm?" I say, trying my best to pretend to be oblivious to what's going on.

"Can you tell me what's brought you here today?"

I shrug, trying to avoid crying, puking or both. Mum is still going strong though; she gets a tissue out of her bag and blows her nose. She decides to continue.

"Yesterday she ran out of school and came home; there was some sort of argument between her and her teacher so she just left. When I came home and started to ask her about it, she lost it with me and started punching herself in the face. I don't know what to do!"

"Hmm," Dr Jackson replies as he starts clicking around on his computer. "The last time I saw you, Luna, was when you were sent for a number of tests around your stomach complaints, and they all came back negative which was good, because what we were testing for was more serious than the diagnosis you were given, which was colic related to stress and anxiety. Do you still have the stomach pains?"

"Sometimes," I tell him "but the sickness is worse now."

Mum butts in. "She used to always say she was feeling sick, but she never actually threw up. I thought there was something going on at school, bullying or what have you, but she swore blind there wasn't. The school ended up contacting me about her attendance because she would say she was ill and I would let her stay at home. I ended up having to send her in because they were threatening me with court action. They asked me if there was anything they could do to help, but there didn't seem to be any problem at school, so there was nothing they could do really."

"I see," Dr Jackson says, looking at me over the top of the glasses that he has pushed down his nose so he can see the computer screen. "How are you outside of school Luna?"

"I don't feel as bad when I'm at home; I still get pains

sometimes though. I think I've got appendicitis," I add, because at one point I thought I did, so I might as well check it out while I'm in here, then I can just go home.

"What makes you think you have appendicitis?" he asks.

"I Googled it."

Dr Jackson smiles at me. "Luna, that's the worst thing you can do! If you were genuinely concerned you had something as serious as appendicitis it's best to be checked by a Doctor. Now let me take you back to the original question, how are you outside of school?"

Damn, I thought I'd dodged that one, thrown him a curveball, but no. He must have noticed. Clever man – well, he is a doctor. I shrug.

"Do you have good relationships with friends, enjoy a social life, that sort of thing?"

"She doesn't go out," Mum tells him. She's *such* a traitor. "She hasn't been out for a while, she just stays in her room, but I've left her to it because she told me that's the way these days, that that's what everyone does now; communicate online, you know? So I just left her to it, even though I had concerns, she seemed happy enough until recently."

"So you think this has escalated recently?" he tries to confirm.

"Well running out of school and punching yourself in the face is hardly normal behaviour is it?" Mum's getting stressed now.

Dr Jackson makes a 'calm down' gesture with his hand and says "We need to remember that Luna is here, Mrs. Jones. I think I need to make another referral," and he starts writing something down. I assume it's going to be for a magic pill but then I realise he isn't writing on his prescription pad.

"Luna, I have to ask you this because of what your Mum has told me, do you have any thoughts of suicide?"

"Sometimes I think I would be better off dead and sometimes I wish I was, but that's it," I say.

"Do you have a plan to take your own life?"

"No, I don't" I answer, and this is the truth. I'm too scared to try and kill myself in any case, so even if I really wanted to I wouldn't. I just wanted this feeling to end. "Is there something I can take, a pill or something?" I ask him, hopefully.

Dr Jackson smiles. "Luna, I'm reluctant to give you any medication at this time because of your age. Given your history of stomach complaints and headaches, and the recent avoidance of school and lack of social activity, I'm inclined to believe that you may have a clinical diagnosis of anxiety. However, I'm not the right person to diagnose that and I'm certainly not the person who can treat you most effectively. I could give you a pill, and that might make you feel better in the short term, however, that wouldn't be ideal. I'm going to refer you to someone who I think will be able to benefit you."

"Who is it?"

"She's a lady called Sadie Rainbow. I've referred patients to her for a number of years and she really is very good at what she does. If she is able to take you on as a client, she will be able to see you fairly quickly, she doesn't keep a waiting list so if she has no space, she'll let me know and I can refer you to someone else. Are you happy for me to make this referral?"

I nod; maybe Sadie Rainbow can give me some pills. Dr Jackson picks up his phone and dials a number. After a few moments he says "Sadie, Roy Jackson here."

I pick at my nails as he explains that he wants to refer a patient to her, and then there are a lot of 'excellent's and 'thank you's so I guess she must have said yes. When he hangs up, he sits forward, leaning on his desk before he speaks.

"We're really fortunate here, Luna, that we have a good working relationship with Sadie and she will take patients from us quite quickly. I know not every GP surgery has such a privilege. She has given me an appointment for you next Thursday at 6.30pm," he starts to write this all down. "It's imperative that you attend and I'd like you to give this a really good go before we start going down the medication route."

Something he has just said resonates with me and wakes me up. What was that? No medication? I thought that was why he was referring me to this Sadie; I thought she would be another doctor who could give me pills to take this all away.

"I don't get it," I quickly tell Dr Jackson before he can announce our time is up and I have to leave not knowing, "isn't this lady a doctor?"

"No she's not, Luna, but she is very experienced and very good at what she does." He's trying to justify it now, trying to make out like it would be worthwhile my going. He must have worked out that I already think this, whatever it is, is going to be a load of crap. Mum looks at the piece of paper he has given her, nodding that she will be able to get me there.

"Well what's she going to do then?" I ask. I'm feeling quite panicked now; this seems to be going horribly wrong and it looks like I'm about to leave the surgery with no cure, no prescription, no pills and no way of getting better.

"She's a counsellor Luna. I'm referring you for therapy."

CHAPTER 8

Mum and I aren't really speaking in the car on the way home. Usually when I go to the doctor's, we stop off at the chemist and collect my prescription and Mum will buy lunch from the bakery next door as a treat because I'm ill. There's no need to stop at the chemist today though because I have been refused my magic pill. I don't think Mum really knows what to say to me; I mean what is the right thing to say when you find out your daughter qualifies for therapy? Maybe she is embarrassed. I think secretly she would have liked me to have a magic pill too, then I could become normal once more and everything would be fine and dandy.

When we come into the house I'm expecting her to go back to work, but she says she is staying home today. I don't know what the point for this is though because now she's downstairs and I have come up to my room, and I'm sure we'll be in separate rooms until dinnertime.

I've decided to trial my potential new job of providing feedback for daytime television, but I have already encountered my first difficulty – I can't actually sit and concentrate on an entire programme. I channel hop for a while catching a bit of this and a bit of that, but nothing holds my interest for longer than two or three minutes. This could form part of my feedback, but it wouldn't contain anything constructive because I can't even suggest improvements to the current viewing schedule. All I can say is that I have found every programme mind-numbingly boring. Maybe I'll have to rethink my plan for the future.

I look out of my window into our back garden. It's only a little stamp of grass and an empty flowerpot that Mum added to brighten it up. It worked when she first put it there, having bought it when the flowers were already in bloom, but that didn't last as they died during the winter and they've failed to re-blossom. Maybe that's what happened to me? Maybe during the course of my normal development a part of me died, and I failed to re-blossom as I should have done? Who knows? Next door's cat is curled up sleeping by our back fence, and I wonder what it must be like to be a cat. Are they happy? Do they have memories? Do they have feelings? When cats get into fights with other cats, has there been an argument? Why do some cats get on with other cats and why do some cats dislike each other and fight every time they cross paths? And are there love triangles in the cat world? Would I like to be a cat? Would I be popular as an animal? I spend a good twenty minutes considering the ins and outs of each of these points before coming to the conclusion that my life is indeed tragic if wondering what it's like to be a cat is my dominant thought, if not the highlight of my day.

I sent Gigi a message earlier telling her to contact me when she is home from school. That'll be soon. I think I will go downstairs and find something to eat and drink so I am prepared when Gigi either voice- or video-calls me.

I am half way down the stairs when the front door opens and Marley walks in.

"Alright?" I say. Notice I say, I don't ask. I don't really care to know if he is indeed alright or not, it's just a form of greeting.

"Yeah, you?" he asks. He must have spoken to Mum. Marley never asks if I'm alright, never.

"Yeah." I have made it downstairs and am heading to the kitchen by this point, Marley walking in behind me. I open the fridge and look inside. As I am debating what to have, though my choice of good stuff to eat is limited, I hear this voice asking me if I want chocolate. My first thought is "Mmm, I *love* chocolate!" closely followed by "That sounded like Marley, I must be hallucinating."

I am still looking in the fridge when a chocolate caramel bar is handed to me. I love chocolate caramel; it's my all time favourite. The hand offering me this divine treat belongs to Marley. Now I could graciously accept the chocolate from this intruder pretending to be my brother, but, no! I am Luna-Ray Jones so I have to get it wrong. Instead I find my best sarcastic voice and ask "will you not need it when you have the munchies later on?"

Marley looks annoyed. "What are you on about?"

"We know you smoke weed, Marley, isn't that what happens to potheads when they've been smoking? Talk a load of crap, annoy everyone, binge on ice cream and go to sleep?" Well, why have a conversation when you can start an argument?!

I regret it immediately as Marley says "I bought it for lunch and didn't eat it, I just thought you might want it. I won't bother asking next time." I hear him mutter "ungrateful cow," under his breath as he turns around and walks upstairs.

"What's gone on now?" Mum says as she walks into the kitchen. "Has he upset you Luna?"

"No, I'm fine."

"I phoned him earlier and specifically told him he was to make an effort because of what the doctor said. I actually thought I'd had a normal conversation with him, I told him we need to get through this as a family and I foolishly believed that he might have understood. I feel so bad Luna, I've spent so long focussing on him, trying to get him to stay at college and work, worrying about him when he's out all hours, that I didn't even notice what was going on with you" and with that she bursts into tears.

Simultaneously I realise two things. First, I have allowed Mum to think Marley is in the wrong here when actually it was me that had caused the problem and now she's wrongly upset with him. And second, Marley was not giving me his lunch leftovers because he hates chocolate caramel, he must have actually bought it for me. So in the space of three minutes and two sentences I've managed to upset my entire family. Good going, Luna-Ray, give yourself a gold star! I am much less trouble when I'm on my own in my room thinking about being a cat.

I leave the chocolate on the side and go upstairs leaving Mum sniffling at the kettle, making tea.

As I get to my door, Gigi pops up on my laptop for a video call. I answer and make myself comfortable on my bed ready to tell her about the events of the day.

After I finished telling her about Dr Jackson and his refusal to give me a pill and instead send me to therapy, Gigi asks "So is that a good thing?"

"Not really."

"What do you have to do in therapy?"

"I don't know. Talk I suppose."

"Will you go?"

"Well I'll have to because I can't get any pills until after I've finished."

"Do you really want pills?"

"No. I hate taking tablets."

Gigi laughs. "What do you think she will be like?"

I haven't given this much consideration until Gigi just said it which is surprising because usually, having had a whole afternoon to think about it, I would have over-thought everything until I knew Sadie Rainbow better than she knows herself, despite the fact I've never met her.

"Probably really old, grey hair, glasses, frumpy dresses, overweight... that's probably it."

"Wow, Luna, you really know how to flatter people! You forgot to add hairy legs and sandals." We both laugh at this.

"I'm glad your Mum knows, Luna."

"Are you?"

"Yeah. I've wanted to tell my Mum for ages so she could tell yours, but I promised you I wouldn't say anything."

I'm a little bit gobsmacked by this. I never realised that I've put pressure on Gigi; I'd never want to do that.

"Would you have said something?"

"I don't know. I've been worried about you; I know you haven't been happy for ages. I just didn't know what to do for the best. Maybe I would have said something, I don't know, but I wouldn't have wanted to give you a reason to hate me either. It's all out there now though. And maybe Sadie won't have hairy legs or sandals."

We both laugh again. "I'm really sorry about the other day, Gigi."

"What are you on about?"

"I suppose it was just hard hearing it out loud that I haven't been normal lately. And then I was annoyed because you dropped me as soon as Jay came online and you went to talk to him."

"Luna, I didn't drop you! I thought you were getting irritated with me going on about him. I do really like him though, so I just wanted to get off the phone to you before I hurt you by being so insensitive talking about him when you're having such a hard time. I wish I could do more, it's so hard being so far away from you and I just didn't know what to do. I kind of worry about making you hate me because I don't know what to say sometimes, I get scared I'm going to say the wrong thing."

"Gigi, you'd never say the wrong thing! I'm the champion of that in any case." I actually really love this girl. I have been so absorbed in her being a friend to me that I didn't even consider she might be bothered about me being a friend to her. It has kind of shocked me too that she was worried about upsetting me. I feel really bad now that I had assumed the worst of her the other day.

"You'll always be my best one, Luna!" Gigi tells me, in the voice of a two-year-old that makes me laugh.

I tell Gigi about Marley buying me chocolate and me being horrible to him and Mum being upset.

"You'll sort it out with them." I hope she is right but I don't know how. I always seem to do this, get myself into situations that I don't know how to get out of. I feel ashamed of myself, but just before I start to get upset Gigi says "Luna would you still be my friend if I looked like this?" And screws her face up so her mouth is twisted and her eyes are squinted.

I laugh again. Gigi always knows how to cheer me up. "Course I would. Would you still be my friend if I looked like this?" and I pull a face at her. We carry on doing this for another half an hour or so, pausing to catch our breath from laughing so much and also adding voices to our new looks.

I'm not sure we will ever tire of this game. We've been playing it since we were eight.

CHAPTER 9

It seems like ages ago that I went to the doctor but it was only yesterday. Today, Mum and I have come to see Mr Davis, my delightful head-of-year. I'm not wearing my uniform because I don't want him to get any ideas that I might actually be staying. I'm definitely going home after this; I can't face the thought of going back to lessons just yet and Mum, for some strange reason, has said that this is OK. She must think I'm bad.

We're waiting in the general office for him to come down and see us. Mum is looking twitchy; I think she might be worried that if I don't come to school she will go to prison or something. Just then Mr Davis walks in with an outstretched hand to greet Mum. He'd better not try and shake *my* hand. Weirdo!

"Mrs. Jones, it's good to see you!" he says, with much enthusiasm. This is an act, I can tell, he's not usually this jolly. I hate it when teachers do this; pretend that they're really nice and really care about you while the parents are about and then as soon as the Mums and Dads have left they go back to their usual not-so-charming selves. "Luna," he looks at me and gives me a sort of nod of the head, without even half of the enthusiasm he greeted Mum with. He must have used up his quota for the day.

"Thank you for seeing us, Mr Davis." Mum said that, I didn't. I'm not in the least bit thankful that I've had to come in here to see him; I feel quite edgy, actually. I feel better that Mum is here with me, but I'm worried that I might be expelled for running out two days ago. That seems more like four years ago now. My head's all over the place, like I've lost all sense of time. In a way, being expelled would be a huge bonus because I would never have to come here ever again, but Mum would be upset and it would probably cause a lot of chaos. I hate not knowing what's going to happen.

"That's quite alright, Mrs. Jones, I think it's good that we have this opportunity to speak together and work out how we can move forward with Luna-Ray. I must say I was quite surprised to hear what happened in Miss Baker's class the other day; I thought it was most out of character." As if to highlight the point a little more, and to prove to me that he must have seen Miss Baker since, he hands me the pencil case and maths book that I had left on the desk when I ran out.

I lean down and drop them into Mum's oversized handbag as she says "I know, I can only apologise for her behaviour Mr. Davis, I still haven't got to the bottom of what happened."

I want to punch them both in the face. This conversation is making me feel a bit sick actually, "Oh, it's *so* out of character!"... "oh! I don't know *what* happened!" ...alright morons I am sitting here you know! Why do people do that? I can't work out what's worse; to have a conversation about someone behind their back or to do it while they're blatantly sitting there in front of you.

I wish I had the ability to say what I really want to say, to tell both of them exactly what happened in Maths the other day, let them know what it's like for me coming in here day after day, tell them what it's like being in my head, but yet again, anxiety wins. I can't work out what I'm feeling myself so I'm hardly likely to be able to explain it to someone else, and even if I could I would need more than the three words anxiety will allow me to project. I feel so trapped; I hate this. I hate it, hate it, *hate* it. And then just as I'm thinking things can't possibly get any worse, anxiety mutters to me "don't be silly Luna, of course they can," flicks the tap switch to my eyes and out of nowhere I begin to cry.

Up until this point, Mum and Mr. Davis have been talking about GCSE's and what subjects I'm taking and the importance of me being in class, they've been talking like I'm not here, but my loud sniffle reminds them that, yes, I am here, and they both turn to look at me.

"Luna, what's the matter love?" That's Mum talking, Mr Davis wouldn't call me 'love'.

I shrug. "I don't know."

"Luna, I understand you went to the doctor's yesterday, can I ask what happened there?" Mr Davis asks.

"She's been referred for therapy, it starts next week." I thought Mum had jumped in and taken over answering for me, but then I realise that I had kind of zoned out for a minute and hadn't actually answered. Mum is trying to make it easier I think; this is a great help for me and I no longer want to punch her in the face. "The doctor thinks she may have anxiety..." she adds, and then goes into a great spiel about what the doctor said, what had happened before when I was referred to him for the stomach pains etc. Mr Davis sits and nods along accordingly in that teacher-y kind of way that only teachers have.

"OK, so in terms of Luna returning to school, have there been any suggestions made as to how we can help her while she is here?"

Mum shakes her head; no, no suggestions. Maybe that will mean I won't have to come back?

"Well, we have worked with students before who have had a diagnosis of anxiety so I have a few ideas of things we can put in place to see if they would help. There's no 'one size fits all' solution and it will be trial and error for us to see what works for Luna, hence why I asked if you have any suggestions."

I've got a great suggestion! Maybe I could work from home four and a half days a week and come in for half a day to speak to my teachers, they can all check that I'm still alive and give me my work and then I can go home again. I don't know if it's fortunate or not that anxiety will not let me speak this idea out loud. It does however decide to let me stop crying and I hope that will be it for now. I know I need to get it together to try and sort this out, so I wipe my eyes and blow my nose, trying to compose myself.

"OK, so the first thing I will do is give you this, Luna." He slides a small rectangular piece of paper across the table to me. It's a nice lavender colour and has 'Time Out' written across the top. "What we need to agree is how we fill the rest of that in." There are two blank spaces, one says 'Time' and the other, 'Place'. "If you need to leave a lesson, Luna, you can use this card. We don't want you running out of the school like last time because we didn't know where you were. We need to keep you safe and it gave us all a bit of a fright because of course, no one could find you."

It hadn't even occurred to me that anybody would look for me. No wonder Mum was keen to run out of the kitchen and call him the other night. I'd been really angry with her for that but now it's starting to make sense. I might apologise for that. Unlikely, but at least I've considered it.

"So how much time out do you think you would need?" I'm hoping he means in hours or days, but I quickly realise that is wishful thinking. "Can I suggest ten minutes?" he says.

"Yeah," is about all I can manage, even though I really want to disagree and suggest an hour.

"So, where would you want to go during that time out? You could come to the year eleven office, there's usually someone around, or you could go to Student Support. Which would you prefer?" I have to think about this, I can't believe I am getting to choose. I decide on Student Support and Mr Davis takes the card back from me, writes the details on there and signs it. "So, if you ever need to get out of a class again Luna, just use this."

"How?" I ask him.

"What do you mean?"

"Well, how do I use it? What do I have to do?"

Mr Davis smiles at me. "That's a really good point, Luna. How would you like to use it?"

I have to give this some consideration. If I hold it up, everyone will know I am going for time out and I don't want people to know. I don't even want people to know that I have the card. We agree that with this in mind, the best thing for me would be to leave it on the teacher's desk when I go into class and then if I need to, I can put my hand up and when the teacher looks at me, I can make a 'T' symbol with my hand, so I don't have to say anything. The teacher will then know that I'm having time out and they will also know that I have ten minutes and will be in student support.

"You might want to have a practice with it." I'd forgotten Mum was even in the room until she says this. Mr. Davis and I both turn to look at her. "Well, you practice the fire bell so everyone knows what to do, Luna can practice her time out so that at least when she really needs it, it's not a new thing and she knows what she's doing. That's alright isn't it?" she tells Mr. Davis rather than asking him, then turns back to me, gently squeezing my arm and says "Have a practice, love." Her enthusiasm about my new time out card made me want to giggle. She has a good point though and Mr Davis seems to agree.

"OK, so we've sorted out leaving class, now we need to work out how best we can keep you in there! Are there any lessons in particular that you find more difficult than others?"

I don't need to think for very long to decide it is maths, especially considering the events of the other day. I don't like Mrs. Baker, I don't like the subject, I don't like anything about it, but I don't think it would be right to share all of this with him so I just say "Maths."

"Well, it's a core subject so we can't withdraw you from it, what would make it easier for you to be in the lesson?" I shrug once more. I don't really know what my options are and I think Mr. Davis picks up on this. "Well, where would you prefer to sit in your lessons, at the front near the teacher, or at the back? Some people prefer to be at the back so there is no one behind them, or near the door or in the middle, what do you think?"

"Near the door I think." Depending on which classroom I am in, this would put me either at the front or back but being near the door feels right because if I need to puke at least I can get out quickly and not have to run past anyone. I've never needed to actually throw up but it worries me that one day I will and I would have to struggle through desks and chairs to get to the door, by which point I probably would have totally humiliated myself. Although I feel proud of myself for thinking of this and coming to a decision, it has also prompted anxiety to remind me about feeling sick and with the thought comes the spin-cycle in my stomach once more. I look at Mum who gives me a little encouraging smile. She's stopped interjecting now; I don't think she had thought of these things before either. It's like a whole new world for her.

"OK, so I will get in touch with all your teachers and tell them that they need to find you a space near the door, is that alright?" I can only nod, Mr. Davis is being surprisingly understanding.

"OK so the final point I have to make Luna, I've requested a report from all of your teachers and it seems that your homework is often late, missing or not to the standard you'd started producing in the classroom." I think of all the times I started a piece of work and then threw it away, all of my beautiful brain-storm outlines that had nothing written on them, just lovely shapes and colours that I spent ages decorating and colouring in. I remember my panic-work, thrown together in the middle of the night just so I have something to produce and all the hours of my life sitting in the classroom not really understanding anything, too awkward to put my hand up and ask. I don't explain all of this to Mr. Davis of course, I just shrug like I don't have a clue what he's on about.

"I think what I'm going to suggest, Luna, is that when work is set, your teacher is to check with you to make sure you understand it. I'll make sure they come over to you so you don't have to put your hand up and ask. They can come to the table and work their way around the class checking out with everybody so you're not singled out in any way, how does that sound?"

"Good," I tell him, because I actually think this is quite fair.

"Luna, I would encourage you as well to please get your work checked regularly by your teachers to make sure you're on the right lines and that you're understanding it and doing the right thing. It's not handing it in to be marked, it's just getting feedback so if you have misunderstood something, they can let you know and equally, if you're doing it well, you know you can continue as you are, does that make sense?" I nod and before I know what I am doing, I actually smile at him.

"When will you be returning to school?" he asks. He had to go and spoil it.

"I thought I'd keep her off for the rest of this week and then she can come back Monday for a new week, fresh start you know?" Get in there, Mum!

"Would you be able to try and come in on Friday?" Mr Davis asks, but no, for once I am going to do what my mum suggests. She's right this time. My face must have said it all. "Monday it is then. If you have any more questions come and see me, Luna, or you can ring me," he offers to Mum. They shake hands again and say goodbye as we get up to leave.

As we walk back through the corridor into the main reception and out to the car park I decide that maybe Mr. Davis isn't so bad. I've stopped wanting to punch him in the face for now, anyway.

CHAPTER 10

The following week, we walk into the waiting room having been buzzed through the front door. A lady is walking towards me and Mum from a corridor to our left.

"Hi, you must be Luna-Ray?" she half says, half asks. I nod. "I'm Sadie."

I look at her, trying to do a brief full-body scan without being too obvious. She's nothing like I expected. She's in her late thirties I'd guess, with long dark hair that falls over her shoulders. She's wearing jeans and a checked shirt buttoned up to the collar. Her wrists are decorated with a number of bracelets with different coloured stones set into each one. She is introducing herself to Mum and hands her a piece of paper, but I'm not really paying attention until she turns and asks "are you ready to come through?"

I look at Mum, trying to telepathically urge her to come with me but she doesn't get the message; she just says "I'll be waiting for you when you've finished." She looks like she's going to cry and gives me an encouraging smile and sort of waves me off; if I wasn't feeling so sick I might have found this dramatic send-off a bit amusing as I'm only going down the corridor.

Sadie points at a door on her left with a sign on it saying 'Room Two' and tells me "We'll be going in here but before we do, let me just show you where the toilets are." I haven't asked her where the toilets are but this is killing time and allowing me to walk around a bit so I don't complain. We walk to the end of a short corridor where she opens another door which reveals a loo and a sink, and then we walk back to Room Two. It's a bit weird, in the room there are two chairs facing each other and a small table in between us but set to the side, on which are set a small clock facing me and a box of tissues.

"Have a seat Luna-Ray, I'll just go and get you some water." Sadie walks out of the room pulling the door behind her but not quite closing it, to go and fetch me a glass of water that I haven't asked for and don't want. Maybe that's why she showed me where the loos were, in case I need to go when I've drunk the water. Who knows? I take the opportunity to look around the room. It is a mint green colour, with a picture of some flowers hanging on the wall. A tall lamp in the corner provides the soft lighting that is necessary since there is no window in here. I sit down on the chair which I know must be mine as there is a holdall next to the other chair so that has to be Sadie's. I try to adjust myself and make myself as comfortable as I can, which is no easy task given the present circumstances. Sadie comes back in then with two glasses of water, placing them both gently down on the table. She sits down and asks "Are you OK?" and I nod in reply. I don't yet trust myself to open my mouth in case I puke.

"I'll be doing some talking first so you can get yourself comfortable and get used to being in this room. Are you feeling a bit nervous?" Another nod is all I can manage. "Me too," she says. That surprises me a bit because she's not supposed to be nervous, she knows what's about to happen and I don't. She must guess my line of thinking because she goes on to say "I always feel a bit nervous when I meet someone for the first time, but I'm also very excited about doing this first session with you and seeing how we get on and if I will be able to help."

She launches into a spiel about confidentiality or something and I nod along at what I hope seem like relevant points, while simultaneously wondering how she would react if I throw up all over this lovely carpet. I just catch the end of her saying "help yourself to tissues if you need them, there's a bin under there..." and she gestures under the table where there is indeed a small plastic bin. She carries on speaking while I sit here thinking about how random some of this stuff is.

I notice her looking at me, waiting for an answer to a question I haven't heard. I give her the blank look, wondering if she's going to throw me out for wasting her time by not concentrating on what she's saying. She doesn't though; she just asks again "What do you hope to gain from these sessions?" OK, I'm with her now.

"I want to feel more confident, I suppose. I want to stop being so anxious and feeling sick all the time."

"Can you tell me a bit about what's been going on for you?" I shrug; I've no idea how to answer that question. Sadie reaches down into the massive bag beside her and pulls a sheet of paper out. "Here, this might make it easier, we can either fill it out together or you can do it on your own if it's easier, what would you prefer?"

"Together," I decide, because it might take longer that way and I can kill some more time.

"OK, so on a scale of one to five where five is great and one is not so good, how would you score yourself on these things?" The questions relate to sleep, eating, feeling confident, angry, worried and stressed, my relationships at home and my relationships at school. I score them all at one or two and feel like a total failure. Sadie doesn't seem to notice how crap my life is, or if she notices she doesn't appear to be fazed by it. Instead she says "so we've got some stuff to work on here. Thank you for being so honest with me."

I half smile then look at the floor. I glance up briefly and see her looking at me so I quickly throw my eyes back down to the floor in case she expects me to say something. "What do you prefer to be called?"

"Erm...Luna I guess..." This is getting weirder by the second, when is she going to fix me?

"This process isn't a quick fix Luna. I'm afraid I don't have a magic wand but I can try and help you to manage these feelings a bit better. Are you committed to doing some stuff in your own time? Practicing techniques I might give you?"

"Yeah," I say, non-committally. The last thing I need is more homework.

"I think a good place for us to start is to talk about anxiety and where it comes from and why in some situations it can be a useful thing to have. Let's go back in time – think of cavemen." I try to look interested but this is a history lesson and I couldn't care about anything less. I want her to fix me not talk about bloody cavemen. She starts and I do my best to focus.

"A caveman would go out and hunt for food. His brain wasn't as developed as ours are now, but what caveman did have, that humans still have now, is the security system, otherwise known as the amygdala. Now this is the most stupid part of our brain system and holds the key to what you might have heard of as our 'fight or flight' response. Do you know about that?"

"Kind of..."

"The security guard, as I call him, senses danger, which then triggers the fight or flight response. We have to either run or fight in order to protect ourselves, ultimately to stay alive. So imagine our caveman, there he goes out on his hunt for food, he's in the woods and about fifty metres or so away, he sees a big grizzly bear which is also looking for its dinner. The caveman's security guard spots this, alerts him to the danger, and this is when the fight or flight kicks in. He doesn't have the thinking brain system that we have, which is good, because there's no time to weigh up the pro's and con's of both running and fighting, he has to choose one or the other really quickly. The adrenaline kicks in to help him; he is probably able to work out that he doesn't have much of a chance if he takes on a bear, so 'fight' is out, and if he goes with 'flight', which he inevitably will, he needs to move quickly, because there's not too much distance between him and the bear, so he needs to be as light on his feet as he can be. So his system has to empty; he will either vomit or empty his bowels to help him get away as fast as he can. Fast-forward a few thousand years and we still have that security guard in our brain, but we're also far more developed in our thinking. What doesn't change sometimes is this – if we find ourselves in a situation where we feel afraid or anxious about something, the security guard will shout 'Danger!' and our physical response can be the same as it was for the caveman. It may result in us feeling sick, having an upset stomach- Does that make sense to you?" I nod affirmatively once more. "So you said you want to stop feeling sick all the time?"

"Yeah," I reply, slightly dumbstruck by what I have just learned. "So is it quite normal to feel sick all the time then?" I ask.

"If you're in an anxious state, yes it can be. Sometimes, the anxious feeling can be with you so often that you start to feel anxious about being anxious and that can be enough to trigger the security alarm. You know how a smoke alarm can go off because you've burnt the toast?" I nod again. "Well, the security system in the brain can be a bit sensitive like that too – like a smoke alarm doesn't know the difference between a real fire and burnt toast, the amygdala doesn't know the difference between a real danger and a false alarm, so it will warn you anyway. Have you ever been in a situation where you have had to use fight or flight, Luna?"

I tell Sadie about the days I have avoided school, the times I have hidden in the toilets and that awful day when I ran from the classroom. She listens to me, not interrupting or telling me off or laughing at me. I realise as we talk that it isn't that my body's not working right, it's just working too much at the wrong times. I still don't know why though, or how I can stop it.

Sadie goes on, "The security guard senses what he thinks is danger, a trigger which could be anything – a sight, a sound, a smell or a feeling, and when this is sensed, the alert is sent out. Now in the brain, there is also a 'Boss', who can go and rest for long periods of time and let the deputy take over. I call her Norma, because Norma sends the messages that become 'Normal' for the person. So Norma assists in sending the familiar messages, repeating the same responses for the same messages. We want this to stop, so we need to get Boss back in to teach Norma the new instruction. Boss will assist with the learning of this and when this becomes the new message, he can go and rest again. So right now, we're at the stuck stage, a state of being anxious a lot of the time because there are no new messages yet and the security guard and Norma are getting in a panic, thinking it's a life-and-death situation."

I am starting to get what she is saying, but one thing is puzzling me. "How do I know what the trigger is?"

"Well that's what we're going to try and find out. It might simply be that it's anxiety about being anxious. In the meantime, we need to calm Norma and the security guard down". Great, here comes my cure. Just as I am getting excited about being made better, Sadie says the most ridiculous thing ever. "Breathing."

"Breathing?" I repeat. This is a waste of my time, I wouldn't be here if I didn't know how to breathe – I mean I *literally* wouldn't be here, I would be dead, so obviously I breathe and I'm still anxious, so what is she going on about?

Sadie must have read my mind because she chuckles and says "I want you to practice a breathing technique. Practice it while you feel calm and use it when you feel anxious." She reaches into her bag and passes me a pot of children's bubble mixture. Does she even know how old I am? "I can see you're not impressed, you don't have to tell anyone." She pulls a pot out for herself and tells me to try and blow a massive bubble. I blow at the bubble wand and the mixture just kind of disappears. Sadie blows a stream of bubbles expertly into the room. "Try again" she says. "Breathe more gently, take your breath from your stomach and breathe out slowly and deeply". I try again and this time produce quite a big bubble but get a massive head-rush at the same time. Sadie carries on blowing bubbles into the room.

"When you start to feel anxious and panicky, your breathing will change. You'll feed the panic with the oxygen you're taking in because your breath will quicken. You're then sending signals all over your body that you're in a dangerous situation and your body will start responding as it thinks it should – Norma will be firing messages all over the place. Breathing can be a huge indicator to the security guard that there is no danger and all is well. So first things first, get your breathing back under control. The bubbles are just to learn and practice with. You'll soon be doing it without the need to have the bubbles in your hand. Then you can count on your fingers, breathe in for two and out for five, then in for three and out for seven or eight. Just practice with it, experiment, see what's comfortable for you. The important thing is that you breathe out for longer than you breathe in."

I carry on blowing bubbles for a while. I notice how the change in my breath is changing the way I am able to blow the bubbles – sometimes I get a long stream, sometimes I get one massive bubble – it is actually remarkably entertaining. I haven't blown bubbles since I was a small child. Sadie lets me keep the bubbles and my 'homework' is to keep practicing.

Time's up and I get up to leave. Sadie and I have both

decided that we will be able to work together so I'm to come back in a week's time. Sadie asks me if I have any questions, which I don't. Remarkably, what she has said really does make a lot of sense and for the first time in months, I kind of feel normal. Well not normal exactly, but I'm beginning to understand what is going on with my body.

Mum's sitting in the waiting room, just as she said she would be. I'd forgotten about her being there to be honest. "You ready Lu?" she asks.

"Yeah," I reply and we leave the building. We walk back to the car in silence. I'm expecting Mum to ask me the ins and outs of everything that has happened with Sadie but she doesn't. There's something funny going on here. It all becomes clear as we get to the car; as Mum puts her handbag down at my feet I notice the piece of paper Sadie gave her earlier sticking out of the top. "What does that say?" I ask her, gesturing at the paper.

"Read it if you like," Mum tells me, so I do.

It's all about turning up to the appointments on time, cancelling appointments with plenty of notice and some other boring stuff, plus the bit Mum is obviously acting out right now, which says "It may be tempting to ask your child lots of questions about their session, but please allow them to come to you and share any details they wish to." Mum will find that really hard! I think I'll be fair and tell her the basics of what we were talking about and I show her the pot of bubbles and explain the breathing exercise.

Mum nods and says "That's nice"; she's struggling, bless her. She likes to know everything, she's annoying like that. She's doing well, considering.

We have a little chat in the car about random irrelevant

stuff but I am glad to be home and in my room so I can have a proper think about what happened this evening. My terrible scores on the score sheets, the fight or flight and how this has been applying to me. It is all starting to make a bit of sense. I ask myself how I feel about it. Relief, that's what I feel. Relief that I am normal as an anxious person and nothing unusual has happened to me. I'm not getting a magic pill, I know that much now, but Sadie has told me that she will be giving me 'techniques' so from that I gather that something will be happening eventually to make me feel better.

I have been sitting by my window blowing bubbles into the night air, watching them float away. Some last longer than others; some pop straight away but others seem to float up and up. I can't work out if they are floating out of sight or popping. I'm tired, that's one thing Sadie said in the opening speech that I didn't pay proper attention to. I must have been paying some attention though because now it is happening I remember her saying it. She told me that sometimes therapy can make you feel very tired and it's normal for that to happen. I get ready for bed, I'll shower in the morning; I can't be bothered to do it now. I collapse into my bed and it's only as I lie here, my eyes closing and my body not fighting it for once that I realise something. It is my last thought before I fall into deep slumber. At some point when I was sitting in the room with Sadie Rainbow, at some point, I'm not sure when, I stopped feeling sick.

CHAPTER 11

I spent the weekend pretty much as usual, or what usual has become recently, which is sitting in my room with my headphones on, listening to music. I didn't slept until late on Friday which meant I got up later on Saturday, much later, as in one o'clock. Then I couldn't sleep Saturday night, had another lie-in on Sunday, went to bed much later and now here I am, bleary eyed on Monday morning. I haven't really spoken to Mum much these past few days either, she must be leaving me alone to think about the fact I have to have counselling because my life is so crap. I'm going to enjoy this while it lasts, which won't be for long I'm sure.

I don't bother going to registration until the last minute, I go to the toilets instead and sit in there for a while. Thankfully no one has come in which leaves me time to sit and think about what today might bring; and that's bound to be something awful. I time my entry to my form room perfectly, making sure I am there just in time to get my late mark in the register, but without enough time to have to actually sit down and do anything. Just as I am about to make my escape Mr. Edison, my form tutor, calls me to stay behind. I am expecting him to be cross with me for being late, but surprisingly he isn't. He says that it's good to see me and that he has spoken to Mr. Davis and when I am ready, I can come and speak to him about what would make it easier for me to be in registration on time every day. I don't say anything and he doesn't ask me to. He just says "when you're ready, Luna," and that's it.

None of my friends are in my form; I sit next to a girl called Joanne usually. She is friends with the girls on the next table so if I do go into the classroom, she doesn't even acknowledge me, just turns her back to me so she can face them and talk. I usually just sit there until the whole painful process is over then I can go to my lessons. Most recently this has translated as me going to the toilets or for a little wander around the school.

I suppose I will have to go and talk to Mr. Edison at some point, but I don't really know what he is expecting me to say. What would make it easier for me to be in registration on time every day? The easiest thing for me would be if I didn't have to go in at all, but I guess that's not going to happen.

I make my way through the corridors to my first lesson, which is English. I used to really like English, I used to like creative writing at my old school but we don't seem to do anything good like that anymore. It's all about reading boring books and analysing them and stuff. I don't even know what analysing means when it comes to books and I don't think it's unusual to struggle with something you neither enjoy nor understand. The English classroom is set out in two blocks of four rows, with the teacher at the front and the door at the back. As I approach, there seems to be a bit of a kerfuffle going on at the door. I can hear Miss Lawson's voice saying "...you here, and we'll have you over there..." It's only as I get to the door that I realise she's changing where everyone sits. I'm going to end up sitting next to someone I hate I just know it. I pretty much hate everyone so it seems like a pretty certain outcome.

As I get to the door she barely looks at me but says "I'll have you here, Luna," and points at the chair at the back and nearest the door. Mr. Davis said this was going to happen, I didn't really believe him though. No one seems happy at having to move chairs so I am probably going to get beaten up at lunchtime when they realise this change around is because of me. Fortunately, no one has been put next to me; there are two boys on the other end of my row but with a space separating us. I think one of them is called Jack, I can't remember the other one's name. I think it begins with 'T' though.

"OK, let's have you all settled then," Miss Lawson says. "Now the reason I have moved you all is because today we are going to be starting a new book, the classic *Of Mice and Men*. It's going to be coming up in your GCSE paper and I wanted for you all to be spending time with different people, getting to learn their ways of analysing and interpreting the text which I hope will challenge some of your thinking, give you a chance to learn some different techniques, that sort of thing. I've tried as best I can to put you with people you may not know so well because as we approach this final piece of learning, your time will be better spent talking about the work and not the weekend." There is a loud groan from across the room which Miss Lawson seems to see the funny side of.

"You'll thank me eventually," she tells the class with a smile.

Just then, the door opens and Amy walks in. I hadn't noticed that she wasn't here before now. "Sorry I'm late Miss," Amy says, panting for breath as if she has been running. She probably hasn't, if she's ever late she sort of strolls to class and then comes in trying her best to look flustered so it appears that she has been rushing, making a big effort to get to lessons.

"No problem, Amy, thank you for your apology, take a seat next to Luna-Ray please."

Amy smiles at me as she sits down beside me. A few people turn to look in our direction but no one says anything, they just turn back round. They are probably all talking about me now, but at least from here, I can see them all and what they are doing. I quite like it. I still feel quite sick, so as the lesson continues I sit practicing the breathing techniques that Sadie has shown me. It kind of helps.

We receive our copies of the new book that we are supposed to be studying and as soon as they are handed out, the familiar feeling of dread starts to set in. I know from past experiences that what will inevitably happen is that Miss Lawson will go round the class and each person will have to read some of the book out loud. I hate this. It is probably one of the top five things I hate about school and I know I won't be able to concentrate from this point because I will be more concerned about when it will be my turn. This won't be for a while because I am now at the back and the reading out loud will start with the people at the front. As I gear myself up for the next forty-five minutes of anxiety-related stress, I'm thinking that the only thing that could get me out of this would be a miracle. And then, one happens! For the first time ever, Miss Lawson offers everyone a 'pass'. If you don't want to read out loud, you can just 'pass' and the next person will carry on. It is *amazing*. By the time it gets to me, four other people have 'passed' and I do the same. It isn't a big deal, it gets to me, I say 'pass' and that's it. It goes along the line to Amy who just takes over and then along the line and so on. I am actually able to concentrate for longer than usual, not the whole lesson, but I don't find my mind wandering half as much as I usually do. I think I might like this topic. When the lesson comes to an end and I pack my things in my bag, I see the 'time out' card lying at the bottom of it, untouched so far. I'd forgotten to hand it in, but actually, I wouldn't have used it in this lesson anyway. I have Maths later, though. I'll probably need it then.

CHAPTER 12

I feel a little better about going to my second session with Sadie, as at least I now know what she looks like and have a slight familiarity with the room. I still want Mum to wait for me though and she says that's OK. I don't know why I want her to be there, but I just feel better knowing that she is.

Sadie walks down the corridor to greet me like she did before, a smile on her face and her hair swishing behind her. She's wearing jeans and a different shirt today, still buttoned up to the collar as it was before, and she's wearing the bracelets again. I can't work out if they are the same ones or not but she is wearing them nonetheless.

"Hi Luna, come through," she says to me while briefly acknowledging Mum. We go to the same room as last time, sitting in the same chairs, same lamp on. "Would you like some water?" Sadie asks. I say no and expect her to go and get herself one but she doesn't, she just sits down. "How are you today?"

"OK, I guess... a bit tired."

"How's your week been?"

This is far more difficult to answer than you would imagine because I don't really pay much attention to how I spend my weeks. I tell her that I have been to school, and I tell her that I still hate school. These aren't long detailed conversations, with lots of ins and outs about the lessons I have been to and the homework I have got; what I actually say is "I've been to school. Hate it." I want to be able to offer more words, but I find it really hard talking in general and even more difficult talking about myself. I don't talk about myself with anyone really so this is a whole new and incredibly difficult experience.

Once again, Sadie doesn't seem to mind. "How have you been getting on with the breathing?" I have actually been practicing that so I am pleased to be able to report back on it without having to make anything up. Mum has even bought me some new bubbles because she didn't want me using up all the washing-up liquid.

"Mum's been supportive of you then?"

I hadn't actually considered this before but I guess she has been. I just thought Mum had bought some bubbles to meet her own need to keep her washing-up liquid supply intact, but she could have banned me from using it and not bought any bubbles so in truth, she has been supportive of me. This is a new way of looking at it and I feel a bit guilty that I haven't thought of this myself. I don't tell Sadie this though. I don't want her thinking badly of me.

"How are you feeling now?"

"Tired," I tell her, which again is the truth.

"How are you sleeping?"

"Not great," I tell her. "I don't think I've ever slept

well."

"What goes on for you at night?" Another question that needs a lot of thought. Why am I finding it so difficult to answer questions about me? It is starting to dawn on me that I don't really think about anything, I just go with the moment which usually involves feeling sick and being worried about something. The worry could be about anything from the past, present or future; worrying doesn't have a time frame of any sort attached to it. I explain how most of the time, I am worried about going to school, so to take my mind off the worrying I usually watch something on my phone or talk to Gigi, maybe play a game on my phone.

Sadie pulls a shocked face and gasps. "Oh, Luna!" she says, pretending to be shocked but I can tell she's messing with me. "You know, they're the worst things you can do if you're struggling to sleep. Watching anything will wake your brain up and playing a game on your phone and using your fingers to tap about will wake it up even more. What's your bedtime routine?"

Well, I don't think I've had one since I was about seven. I am struggling to think of what to say and Sadie helps me out by rephrasing the question "Do you have any kind of routine at all when it's time to sleep?" I tell Sadie how actually I spend quite a lot of time lolling about on my bed, I'll shower when I can be bothered, sometimes before I go to sleep, sometimes when I get home from school. Sometimes I sleep at 9pm, other times I'm awake until 3am. Sometimes I'll go and get something to eat, sometimes I won't. Now that I think about it, I think the only routine is that I slept in the same bed every night.

"Hmm, do you think you could do something about

that?" she asks, "It's so important that you get your sleep." I guess I am willing to try but I don't really know where to start.

We talk through different ideas and things that might or might not work. I say a definite 'No' to camomile tea and I don't really like baths, I prefer showers, so that's a 'No' too. We agree that I will have a starting point – Sadie says there is no point in me deciding that I will try and sleep every night by 9pm; my sleep patterns are so erratic, I would be setting myself up to fail. She says goals must be achievable and realistic, so 11.30pm is the starting point. I'm going to try and be asleep by 11.30pm every night. I'm going to try and shower at the same time each night, get into my pyjamas, spend some time downstairs with Mum and then when I go back upstairs, no more phone. I can read books only, no more games, chatting to Gigi or scrolling through anything on my beloved phone. I might actually die from phone deprivation! I tell Sadie of my fears and she says I can have my phone in my room, but to put it further away from me so I can't easily get to it.

I'm going to keep a sleep diary as well so I can see my patterns. I have to record what time I get up, what kind of day I've had, how much exercise I do, what I eat and drink, what time I fall asleep and how many times I wake up during the night. I say I will start it on Monday because I don't like things starting in the middle of anything and as it is Thursday, it would be too awkward to start from tomorrow. I nearly get away with it, but after prolonged negotiation and Sadie being persuasive, we agree that the weekend can also be construed as a beginning so I will do it from Saturday. This woman drives a hard bargain.

Then we talk about exercise. Now I walk to and from school which takes about fifteen minutes each way, but apparently, I need to do more. At first I wonder if Sadie is making a dig at my weight, but it turns out that actually, exercise is going to be an important part of helping me to not feel anxious. "It releases the feel-good chemicals our body needs. Did you ever see someone looking disappointed with themselves when they finished a workout? They might not look like they're having the greatest time while they're doing it, but when you finish it's a sense of achievement." My biggest fear here is that I am so unfit, and I confide in Sadie that I'm not sure I'll be able to manage more than seven minutes of exercise. Sadie just says "Start with doing seven minutes then. And maybe the next time you'll be able to do eight." Sounds fair.

"OK, now let's talk about how we can manage this worrying Luna." As she says it, I think that with everything she just said about goals and being realistic, she might have realised that getting me to stop worrying, is not a realistic goal. It just won't happen. Poor Sadie. Setting herself up to fail. She should listen to her own advice. "It would be pointless me telling you not to worry, because that would be asking the impossible."

Well that shut me up. I'm not going to let her know that though.

"Of course you're allowed to worry, but worrying the day away can leave you feeling more anxious and quite stressed. I wonder, do you know what it is you worry about most?"

"Usually school, friends...what I'm doing with my life," I tell her.

"OK, what I'd like you to try Luna is to write down what

your worrying about as soon as it comes into your head. A 'worry list' if you like. Acknowledge you've had that thought, and you can park it until your designated 'worry time'. This means you can choose what time you worry and where, so it can be in your bedroom or another room in your house, in the garden, wherever you like. But not bed; bed is completely out of bounds for 'worry time'. You can worry beside your bed if you like, but not in it. Bed is for rest and relaxation, not worrying. Then, you can have fifteen minutes of pure 'worry time'. You can pull your list out and worry yourself away with all the things on the list. If you finish worrying before the fifteen minutes is up then great, but you can't have one second over. If you haven't finished worrying, you can add it to the list and worry the next day. How does that sound?"

Well, actually, I think I'd need longer than fifteen minutes, and I tell her so. She won't budge though. Fifteen minutes it is then.

"What I'd also like you to consider Luna is when you look at the list, what is it on there that is worth worrying about now? Will it matter in five years time? What belongs to you? What can you actually do something about now? If you come to a conclusion, a way to resolve that worry or a plan to resolve it, then write it down. Then when you go back to your list, you can see that you've identified a way of moving forward through that particular situation. Does that make sense?"

It does. I have loads to do now! I decide that in addition to my worry list and sleep diary, I am going to keep a comprehensive diary of every move I make as well. I'm feeling quite good about this actually. I can do this! We talk about sleep and exercise some more and then the session is over. I can't help feeling a bit cheated. I still feel quite anxious, I was hoping it would be gone by now.

CHAPTER 13

It was ironic that when I came home from counselling the other day, I didn't have any problem falling asleep. I felt so tired, I got into bed and I was out for the count. On Friday, I started my worry list in preparation for today as Saturday can now be considered as the beginning of a new week, thanks to Sadie and her constant badgering.

It's now 5:30pm and I have managed to waste another day doing not a lot really – well that's not strictly true, I have done some history homework and I've put it in my bag and left it for 'feedback'. As I've been lying on my bed, my school bag has caught my eye once or twice and I've had to really restrain myself from taking my work out and criticising myself about it. I really need to try and forget about it, but the more I try forgetting about something, the more I seem to remember it. I was going to wait until later to start this 'worry time' (which won't work because fifteen minutes is not nearly enough) but to take my mind off worrying about my homework, I need to do something else, and I'll end up worrying in general. With this in mind, I take my worry list and add 'History homework' to the bottom of it. There, I'm ready. Now I need to consider my list and decide what I can do something about now, and what is actually worth worrying about. Here goes:

1. School
2. Having no friends when I'm older
3. Having no social life when I'm older
4. Being embarrassed about being asked for ID in a pub if I don't have any ID
5. The financial crisis
6. Getting a job
7. Passing my driving test
8. How to drive a car
9. Crashing my car
10. Where will I live when I move out
11. What am I going to eat when I move out, I can't cook
12. Mum dying
13. Me dying
14. Marley dying (not a real concern but I suppose I would be upset)
15. History homework

As I look at my list, I'm slightly concerned about myself. I didn't really realise before what exactly I was worrying about, so looking at it is a bit peculiar. But I'm doing what Sadie asked me to do, I've added these items randomly as the thoughts have popped into my head. So I need to decide what I can worry about *now*, what is actually relevant to me. Item one can stay. Items two to eleven don't qualify, as they are not relevant to now. Items twelve to fourteen, I need to consider. I haven't known anyone who has died, however, there's no real reason to think that any of us are on the Grim Reaper's hit list to leave this earth any time soon, so I guess that's just depressing and unnecessary; maybe I should leave these out too. Fifteen can stay, so my new list looks like this:

1. School

2. History homework

OK so this is a little shorter now, but I'm pretty sure that fifteen minutes still won't be enough. I sit on my chair in front of my dressing table and set the stopwatch on my phone. Go!

I have a worry about school. It's a lot more difficult than I thought it would be, because I'm not really sure what I should be worried about. The teachers have all been fine with me lately, I'm more comfortable where I'm sitting and I've done really well getting to and staying in lessons. I haven't actually had to use my time out card yet, which is great. I've been hanging round with the girls at break and lunch and even though sometimes I still only give one or two word answers to things, they seem to be alright about it. I mess around with them sometimes playing 'Hot or Not' which is usually really funny. I smile to myself as I remember sitting with them at lunch yesterday as Poppy and Amy nearly had a full scale argument about which one of them Ed Sheeran was most likely to marry, and Tara and I just couldn't hold our giggles in. It was very entertaining. However, this is 'worry time', and these aren't worries.

I move on to history homework. I've done it; I have something to hand in. The agreement I have is that I will hand in what I've done to get feedback; the actual deadline for the finished piece of work is next Thursday so I will still have time to re-do it if I need to. Or I might not need to, I will know on Monday when Mr. Lee looks at it. I guess this is more like a worry for Monday then.

I'm a little disappointed that worry time seems to be over, and I can't actually think of anything that I really need to worry about right now. I was hoping to use all of my time just to prove to Sadie that I needed much longer than fifteen minutes. I hit the stop button on my phone and look at the timer. It must be broken. I know it isn't broken, but I was convinced that I'd be sitting here for much longer than two minutes and twenty eight seconds. Well, it is what it is. I'll have to start on a new list.

I go downstairs to see what everyone is doing. I find out that Marley is at work; he works in a supermarket a couple of nights and some weekends. I don't really know what he does, he just gets some money in while he's at college doing something a builder does, bricklaying or something; I'm not too sure. Mum is washing up. I walk into the kitchen and take the tea towel from the side and start to dry the dishes she has washed.

"Are you feeling alright, Luna?" she asks me with that voice parents generally use when they're taking the mick out of you but trying to be funny at the same time. I wish she wouldn't, it makes me want to throw the towel at her, give her the two fingered salute and go back to my room, but instead I take a bubble breath, plant a smile on my face and say "Yeah I'm fine thanks, how are you?"

"I'm okay," she tells me, but she has a suspicious air about her, like I'm after something or have been cloned. She's a character, my mother. "How's school going?"

I dry the plate I'm holding much more thoroughly than I really need to while I think about how to answer her. Part of me wants to give her a full answer, but I can't really be bothered because school is my least favourite subject so I settle for "It's alright," which I'm proud of because it's a whole word longer than my usual response of "fine".

"I'll put the radio on, cheer things up a bit," Mum tells me as she does just that. Of course she's chosen a rubbish radio station that's playing some music from about three hundred years ago (well, the eighties I think, same thing) and she starts bopping around the kitchen telling me it reminds her of her youth. It's really weird to think of Mum ever having been my age and I decide that now would be a good time to ask her about it, so I do.

"Well, we didn't have mobile phones back then, we came home when the streetlights came on...all the kids on our street used to go out and play together, you know ball games and bikes, not a computer in sight. Those were the days!"

"Did you play ball games when you were my age?"

"Yeah, I loved it! We used to play kerby, we would go to the park and meet up with the boys from a few streets away, there was a youth club we went to... it was set up to show young people they could have a good time without alcohol, but we used to get drunk on the way there..." Mum rambles on for a bit about her misspent youth while I continue drying dishes wondering why I started this conversation. She's in full flow now but I've sort of switched off.

"Did you ever worry about anything Mum?" I ask her.

"Well yes of course I did!" Her voice suggests that she thinks I'm mad for even asking.

"What kind of things did you worry about?"

Mum rests her hands in the washing up water while she thinks. Eventually she says "Do you know, I can't really remember."

I can't quite get over that, and I wish that this could be me in a few years. That someone would ask me what I used to worry about, and those worries were so far away, that one of my favourite three-word responses would come into play very truthfully and I could tell them "What did I worry about? I don't know."

CHAPTER 14

The room is much more familiar now. Even so, as I walk in today I notice a clock on the wall behind me for the first time. I knew there was a clock in front of me, but I hadn't noticed the other one before. I ask Sadie if it has always been there and she tells me it has. I'm a bit surprised to be honest because I thought I noticed everything, but maybe I don't.

"Is there anything you specifically want to talk about this week?" Sadie asks. There are loads of things I could talk about, loads of things I want to say, but I just don't have the words. I suddenly feel totally overwhelmed and with no warning, no time for preparation, I start to cry.

"It's OK Luna." She doesn't say anything else, just sort of sits there looking at me. The tears continue to pour down my face for what feels like forever, even though it must only be a few minutes. I reach forward to my right and grab at some of the tissues from the box. I dry my eyes, blow my nose, compose myself then cry some more. I don't even know why I am crying. I don't know what I am going to say when it eventually stops. Eventually, somehow, it does.

Sadie looks at me. "If your tears could talk, what would they say?"

"I don't know," and that's the absolute truth. I think for a few seconds. I want to be able to explain, to give reasons, to understand all of this myself but instead I just repeat "I don't know."

"That must be difficult, the unknown."

"It is!" Suddenly I feel validated. She isn't telling me that I should know, she just seems to understand. It makes sense to me as well; of course the unknown is difficult, hard, frustrating.

"Do you have any more words that could describe that feeling?"

"Frustrating," is the one I choose to offer.

"What frustrates you about it?"

"Everything. I don't know why I'm the way I am. I wish I wasn't. I wish I was normal like everyone else, I wish I could do normal things, but I just can't."

"What kind of 'normal' things would you like to be able to do?"

"Well, go into school and sit in a classroom. Go out with my friends without worrying all the time. Be able to join in and not feel like a total freak."

Sadie nods like she was expecting me to say all of this. "Can you tell me about school generally do you think?"

"Yeah....what do you want to know?"

"Whatever you can tell me. Have you ever enjoyed it?"

I think back. I can't really remember much about it from when I was younger, but I know there wasn't some big event that triggered my anxiety. I used to go every day, no problems.

Sadie pulls out a pen and paper from her bag. "Let's do a timeline." She draws a single line across the paper and marks it with a cross at one end. "This is where you are today," she says pointing at the cross. "What can you remember before now? About anything, absolutely anything. What comes to mind?"

I think about it, I don't want to put anything stupid on there and get it wrong. I have to think of something relevant. "I remember changing schools," I say.

"How old were you then?"

I moved to secondary school when I was eleven, so I tell her and she writes it on the timeline. "How did you feel about changing school?"

"I thought I was excited at first, like I'd outgrown primary school. Everyone in my year was really happy and I bounced off them I suppose. But when it came to going, I realised that I didn't want to. That I'd just been copying everyone else who seemed excited, but it wasn't what I wanted. I was really scared, but I never told anyone. Everything was bigger, I didn't know any of the teachers, I didn't know my way around, I wasn't going to know most of the people there; I just didn't want it to happen, I didn't want to go."

"It was a big change. What about your friends?"

Gigi moved away that summer holiday. She was the one I was closest to and I was desperately sad that she wouldn't be coming to the same school as me. I wouldn't even be able to hang out with her after school, she was leaving me completely. Sadie listens as I describe what happened and then writes it on the timeline, just in front of the school change.

"Can you remember anything else?"

I add a few random things; going to the theatre in London with Mum last year, a family holiday we had altogether when I was about ten, a few things I did with Gigi, like going to the park or shopping in the town. Sadie looks at the timeline. It looks a bit pathetic to me; I still think there ought to be a big event on there to justify why I feel the way I do, but there isn't.

"When did you start feeling anxious?" I don't even know why she's asking me this, she already knows I don't know, and that's what I tell her. "That's OK." Sadie points at the timeline around the points where she's written about me and Gigi going out and stuff. "Do you remember ever feeling anxious around these times? Do you remember ever saying you wouldn't be able to go into town with Gigi?" This is interesting, because actually, I don't. I never felt it then.

Sadie draws with a green pen all the way along the line, up until that point. "What about in-between Gigi leaving and starting the new school?" I think back. I didn't really do much around that time, but I thought it was because Gigi wasn't there. Mum asked me a couple of times if I wanted to go out to dinner or to the cinema and I'd said no. I remember hearing her on the phone to Gigi's mum saying that I was in mourning. It was around then that I had started going to the Doctor with the stomach pains. I tell Sadie all of this. She continues the line with an orange pen.

"Did you start the new school when you were meant to?" I had done. I used to go, it had been sort of alright when I first started – everyone was new and anxious I guess. It was just that everyone else seemed to settle in and find their way and I didn't. It was at the start of the year after that it had all gone really wrong and I started skiving. When Sadie hears this she reaches into her bag and takes out a red pen and traces over the original line with the red. She turns the timeline round to show me. She has added 'Started year eight' onto the timeline, just above where the red line starts.

"OK Luna, does this look right to you? Here we have a green line which represents when you didn't really feel any anxiety. When Gigi left, we move into the orange where the anxious feelings were starting to present and you went to see the GP, but you were still functioning, still able to do the things that were expected of you. Move into year eight and this is when the anxiety peaked and the feelings started to become unmanageable, you began to avoid things you were supposed to be doing, like going into class. Up until this point, you were starting to avoid things that weren't absolutely necessary, like going out with your mum for instance, so it probably wasn't as noticeable as it became when you were starting to avoid going into classes and stuff. Does that seem right to you?" Sadie pauses looking at me, still showing me the timeline. "Luna, are you alright?"

I look at the paper and look at Sadie. How long have I spent feeling like a total failure because I don't know when this started, or what went wrong with me? How long have I spent thinking that I've felt like this forever? This woman, who I only met two weeks ago, draws a single line on a piece of paper and works it out in approximately thirty-eight minutes.

CHAPTER 15

I sit on my bed staring at the timeline. Sadie asked me if I wanted to take it with me so I did. Now I'm just sitting looking at it, the answer to one of my big 'I don't know's is now staring me in the face. What Sadie pointed out was that I have spent more of my life without anxiety than I have with it, which is something I now have to get my head around. The other thing that has been quite profound is the realization of when it became unmanageable. At one point I felt like this and coped with it, and now I can't. I remember her saying that we would never want to shut anxiety off completely, just find a way to manage the feelings. I just wish I knew what changed. I've decided I will try and find the answer out at our next session. In the meantime, I want to discover what else I can put on this timeline; I've lived for fifteen years and I have seven things I can remember.

I go downstairs, timeline in hand. Mum is ironing; she always does the ironing on a Saturday, saving it up all through the week for a grand 'iron-athon' at the weekend. I feel a sudden surge of love for her, watching her standing there, her back to me as she attempts to do squats while she irons. She's always going on about her 'admin arse', an occupational hazard she calls it, as a result of sitting down all week in front of a computer.

In my recent twenty-three month (as I now know it to be) state of not coping with anxiety, I'd forgotten to think about Mum. I haven't really appreciated her and everything she does, everything she has always done to keep me and Marley in the lifestyle to which we have become accustomed. We don't live like kings by any means, but there's always food in the house, our clothes are always washed and ironed, there's always hot water and we've never missed out on birthdays or at Christmas. One year, I remember Mum bringing home these cards and envelopes, thousands of them. Every night when Marley and I went to bed she would stay up until the early hours putting the cards and envelopes into a cellophane packet ready to be displayed in the shops. They were Christmas cards and Mum said she was doing it to help her to pay for the big day. I remember telling her that she didn't have to do it because Father Christmas would come with presents, and she told me that Santa would not be paying for dinner, decorations, the tins of chocolates, the tree or the stockings and that was why she had to do it. She also added that "Father Christmas will really treat you this year if he sees you both being really good and going to sleep without any fuss so I can get on with this."

She was right. That year Father Christmas brought me and Marley new bikes; a beautiful pink one for me and a BMX for Marley. We had to wait until after 8am when we'd had breakfast to go out and ride them, we weren't allowed out at 4am when we woke up and had discovered them propped against the lounge wall covered in masses of paper and ribbons. I smile to myself as I make my way into the living room to get a pen so I can make this addition to my timeline.

"What are you smiling to yourself about?" Mum asks as I come and sit on the arm chair in front of her.

"I was just thinking about that Christmas when you got me and Marley bikes, do you remember?"

Mum stops ironing for a minute to look at me. A small smile creeps onto her lips. "Yeah, I remember."

"Do you remember all the cards you packed to pay for them?"

Mum pretends to shudder. "Cor, do I ever?! I stayed up until two a.m., four nights a week for nearly three months, paper cuts all over my fingers, matchsticks to keep my eyes open at work the next day – never again!" She laughs and carries on ironing, then her eyes flick in my direction and she asks "What have you got there?" before looking away quickly to pretend she isn't really bothered if I tell her or not.

"Oh, it's a timeline Sadie and me were doing today. That's why I came down here actually; to ask you what else could go on here." I show Mum what I have done so far.

"Have you only just started it?" she asks in all seriousness. I consider lying but then I figure that this would only be counter-productive.

"No, this is all I can really remember," I say, and I go on to explain the meaning behind the green, orange and red lines. Mum looks down at Marley's shirt on the ironing board, her expression one of sadness. "You OK, Mum?"

"Yeah! Course!" She replies, although I can tell this is a lie because the high pitch of her voice and her now overly bright expression give her away entirely.

"Do you remember going to the drama group on a Saturday morning?"

I smile. How could I have forgotten about that? "Oh yeah, we did Oliver Twist!" I say. "Oh, and I won the booby prize in the raffle – a bag of gruel."

We laugh together at the memory. Mum was so excited to have won in a raffle, she skipped up to the raffle table to claim her prize, spent ages looking at the bottles of wine and boxes of chocolates to see which one her number was attached to and eventually saw that her number was the one stuck to the porridge oats, which was the gruel. Marley and I had spent the next few weeks re-enacting the great moment. "Oooh, look I've won!" Marley would say in a high pitched girly voice (totally unnecessary, he could have used his own which hadn't broken yet) then I would run into the kitchen and grab the most crap-looking object I could find and he would feign great sadness, shock and surprise at discovering his win consisted of a tin from the cupboard or a used potato peeler. Sometimes he would make a generous speech of acceptance, other times he would have a breakdown, bursting into great sobs and throwing himself around on the floor, either of which I would find utterly hilarious. Thinking back now, it seems so clear in my mind, why hadn't I been able to remember it? I guess it was quite important too, because Marley and I actually got on then. We used to go out on our bikes and people would comment on what a lovely brother and sister we were, mainly old people did anyway. We'd go to the shops together on Saturday sweet day with our pocket money and choose from the pick and mix in the newsagents.

"I'm going back upstairs now," I tell Mum as I make my way up to my room. I'm starting to feel sick. Between my memories and my timeline, something is stuck in my head but I can't work out what. I feel really sad all of a sudden and want to cry.

I lie down on my bed. Bubble breaths, that's what I need. I take my pot of bubbles from my dressing table and start to blow. First only one or two rubbish bubbles make their way into the room, but soon I am in a rhythm and the bubbles are coming thick and fast. I know. I knew I knew, but I didn't want to admit I knew. I remember the argument. Not the whole argument, just one line of the argument. I don't know how it started, but I certainly knew how it ended. Marley and I were never quite the same after that. That's the point when we suddenly we could only get along for about twenty minutes a year. I carry on blowing bubbles, the tears escaping from my eyes and onto my cheeks. I don't have to look at the timeline; I know exactly where the argument will fit in. Why did I have to remember this now? I stop blowing bubbles and look at the timeline. I was right, the argument would have happened just there. Just before the green line turns orange.

CHAPTER 16

I've been thinking all week about the new information on my timeline. I've hardly slept and if you can't tell from my terrible skin or the bags under my eyes, then my sleep diary will prove that this has *not* been a good week for sleeping, or eating for that matter. I'm talking through this with Sadie, exploring what happened on what days, looking for patterns in the diary. The only pattern is that there's a big worry on my mind and I have been going over and over it every night. Now it's time to talk about it, I don't know if I want to, but I know that if I don't, I can say goodbye to sleep for the foreseeable future. I sit in front of Sadie and prepare to speak. This will be the first time I have said it out loud to anyone and I am afraid of what it might sound like. I show Sadie the timeline and show her the latest addition to my pointless life.

"Are you able to talk about the argument with Marley?" she asks, and I take a deep breath before answering.

"We were arguing about something. I've thought and thought about it, but I can't remember what started it. Marley was really pissed off with me and he told me that the reason

Dad left and we moved up here away from everyone was because of me. He said it was because I've always been a horrid bitch and that's why he left, I drove him away."

"How old would you have been, Luna?"

"Twelve or thirteen I suppose."

"And Marley would have been....."

"Fifteen or sixteen I think."

"OK..." Sadie leaves this hanging in the air for a few seconds before asking if I can tell her about Dad. All I really know is that his name is Dave Jones, he is a year older than Mum and he still lives down South, I think. He left when I was a baby and we moved up here. I know what he looked like because Mum had a photo of her wedding day that she keeps in her drawer and I accidentally found it one day when I was about thirteen. I wanted to ask her about him but I didn't because then she might have found out that I'd looked in her drawer and she would assume that I had been snooping, even though I wasn't. Well I was, but I was snooping for her secret stash of mints, I hadn't expected to find the photo. I relay this limited amount of information to Sadie.

"How do you feel about your Dad, Luna?"

"I don't know." I feel a bit embarrassed. Sadie is nice and all, but she is still quite a stranger really, and I've just admitted something to her that I have never told anyone before; partly because I was ashamed and partly because I only really remembered the details a few days ago.

"Have you ever spoken to your mum about this?"

I say "No" through what I think is a laugh, but then I realise I am actually crying. "I couldn't tell her I know. She might have forgotten and then I'd remind her and she'd remember to hate me too and then she'd probably leave as well." I'm really crying now; big, fat tears are rolling down my face, dropping onto my jeans. I am almost choking on my sobs.

"I'm a bad person," I manage to get out whilst choking on my words, gasping for air as I do. My chest starts really hurting; I must be having a heart attack! This is my punishment, a heart attack that is going to kill me right here in this room. Just when I think I am about to take my last breath, I see Sadie crouched in front of me.

"Luna, sit nice and straight in your chair for me please, feet firmly on the floor." Sadie's voice is firm but still kind. I try to sit up in my chair but am concentrating mainly on how to stay alive. "Luna, I want you to start your breathing now, try and breathe in for one and out for seven, are you ready? Use your fingers to count on. Ready? Breathe in and out 2,3,4,5,6,7, and again..." Sadie carries on counting while I try to focus on my fingers.

"You're safe now, Luna, stamp your right foot for me and out 2,3,4,5,6,7" Sadie keeps counting while I try to breathe, I'm managing up to four right now. Sadie is looking in her bag for something. "Keep breathing 2,3,4,5,6,7" she continues as she opens a small sealed tub and holds it out in front of me. I look, it's full of buttons. "Can you find five green buttons for me 3,4,5,6,7...."

I start pushing the buttons around the tub looking for the green ones. I can find every other colour, but not green. Sadie is still counting as I find the first green one, then another. I keep rummaging until I find three more. It's only when I'm sitting with five green buttons in my hand that I realise I haven't died.

"Would you like some water?" Sadie asks as she hands me the glass. I guess she means I should drink some anyway. My breathing is now returning to normal and my heart has stopped pounding so viciously, but still it's beating faster than it probably should. I feel like such an idiot.

"The thing with panic, Luna, is not to feed it. The oxygen you breathe in will feed it and can encourage it to get bigger. In a moment of panic, try not to breathe in so much and concentrate on pushing that breath out. Stamping is good because it's grounding. It reminds you that you are here now, not back there, hearing those words or whatever it was that triggered it."

"Why did you need the buttons?" I ask, offering them back to her.

"I didn't. I just needed you to find them. Panic is the emotional brain response; the rational-thinking brain has gone off somewhere, but if we can get the rational-thinking brain back, it can balance the feelings out again. Asking you to find the green buttons switched your focus to a practical task which needed your thinking brain to come in and help you do it."

This sounds quite helpful, but I can see a little problem with it. "So do I need to carry a box of buttons around with me in case it happens again?"

"No, you can use colours, objects, anything around you. If you are in a supermarket, colour is a good one – find five orange lids or six green vegetables, five packets of soup or whatever. Or you could look for whatever is around you, wherever you are and find something that you can hear, see, smell, touch and taste. That's good for reminding you that you are in the moment, this is where you are."

"What if I find them and it hasn't helped?"

"Find five more. Keep breathing, keep stamping. If it goes on for longer than a few minutes, then it's not a panic attack." Sadie pulls out a sheet of paper and gives it to me. "Here you go, it's all on here. It might be useful to give your Mum a copy if you want, just so she knows what to try and do as well."

"Thanks," I say, and take another few sips of water.

"Did you want to carry on talking about your dad today?"

"There's nothing else to say really, the reason he left was because of me." I begin to quietly cry again.

"I wonder Luna, what stops you from asking your Mum what happened?"

"I told you, she'll remember to hate me."

"What if what Marley said wasn't quite correct?"

I had thought of this before, but I don't want to risk hearing it from Mum, because then it would be really true. I explain this to Sadie.

"How would it be different though?" it is her turn to look puzzled.

"What do you mean?"

"Well if your mum tells you the same thing and confirms what you believe to be true, it won't change anything. You'd simply hear the same information from a different person. Would that really change how you feel about it? It's nothing new. Whereas if your mum was to tell you something different....." Sadie waits for me to fill in the blank. It takes me a few seconds to find my three words.

"It changes everything."

CHAPTER 17

I've been trying to find the right time to talk to Mum for the past three days. Sadie's words have been ringing in my ears like a bad case of tinnitus, forcing me to hear them over and over again. How can I really know the truth of why Dad left? I can't trust Marley completely and Sadie is right – if Mum confirms that I was the reason Dad left, it wouldn't change anything.

I cautiously approach the living room door; I don't want to back out now. Mum is on her knees polishing the coffee table with such vigour I think it might collapse. She looks up as I walk in.

"Hey babes, just working on my bingo wings," she says as she flaps her arms around in my face to prove she has excess fat there. The woman is obsessed, she isn't even big, only a size fourteen.

"Mum I need to talk to you." My voice wobbles as I speak. She must hear this because she get ups and walks over to me with her arms outstretched ready to hug me. She pulls me down onto the sofa next to her.

"What's up love?" My palms are sweating and I am glad to sit down as my legs are starting to shake.

"Why did Dad leave?" The words have left my mouth before I've had a chance to think about them – probably for the best or they may have gone unsaid for the next few years too.

Mum's expression has kind of frozen on her face. "What's brought this on?" Her tone is gentle, but even so I want to back out of this conversation already. She is probably being kind because of what she is about to tell me, to soften the blow. I feel embarrassed, I wish I hadn't started it, but still here we are, so I suppose it best just to carry on.

"Well, I was wondering, did he leave because of me?" I watch as Mum's mouth drops open, shock written all over her face. She's probably never thought I'd find out and is quite astonished that I have. She catches her breath and closes her eyes.

"God, no! Where did you get that idea from?"

"Marley told me."

"When?" she asks, her expression quite unreadable now.

"A few years ago," I tell her. Mum lets out a half laugh, half sob that sounds like a bit of a snort.

"Luna, have you thought that for all this time?" I nod. "Oh babes," she says moving closer to me to give me a hug. "No, no, no, that's not true at all!" she tells me as she cuddles me and strokes my hair. "God, I've made a mess of this haven't I?" she says to herself as she sits back turning herself to face me. "The reason me and Dad split up was because he was having an affair." Now it's my turn to look shocked.

"An affair?"

"Yes he was seeing someone else behind my back." I don't

actually need her to clarify what an affair is for me, I know that bit; I want her to tell me more. "Are you sure you want to know all of this?" I nod again, maybe a bit too eagerly, but I'm desperate to know more about the man I don't remember.

"I loved your dad, Lu, I really did; I thought we'd be together forever. When he started coming home from work later and going off on his own at the weekends, I never suspected anything because I trusted him. I think that was the worst thing, why I felt like such a fool, because it never once crossed my mind that he would be seeing someone else. It all came out not long after I'd had you. He told me he still loved me, still loved you kids, but he wanted to be with someone else. He even said he was leaving me in a decent way, because he hadn't walked out while I was pregnant with you, and for that I should have been grateful. Bastard."

There's a pained expression on her face.

"Did you know her, the other woman?" A thousand questions have come to my mind but this is the one that I say out loud.

"Know her?!" Mum's face turns into a scowl. This isn't an expression she wears often, she reserves it for special occasions and hideous people; this woman is obviously on that list. "Oh I knew her alright. She always wanted everything I had, always had to be the centre of attention; nothing was ever good enough for her. She always wanted to put me down, and couldn't bear to see me happy."

"Who?" I ask. Mum is talking like I should know who she is on about. She turns to face me.

"My sister."

"Auntie Alice?!" It's Mum's turn to nod. She closes her

eyes again. "It was a nightmare Luna, it really was. I didn't know how I was ever going to get over him. It was only you and Marley that kept me going, kept me functioning. They moved in together you know; he wanted joint custody of you two. Well I wasn't having that – over my dead body. When he first left he didn't come and see you for the first three weeks, said he was giving me time to adjust and get used to the new situation. Marley was crying all the while, he didn't cope at all well; he was close to his dad. You didn't know any different, you were only three months old. And there I was left to get on with it. When he visited the first time, he only stayed for five minutes and afterwards Marley cried for three weeks. It was when I told him I wanted money from him, that's when he said he wanted full custody of you two. So I did what any mother would do in that situation."

"What was that?!"

"Well, I packed our stuff and moved here, left no forwarding address, nothing. My parents were useless. Alice was always the favourite – spoilt little cow she was, and probably still is. They told me I'd have to get used to it and find a way to be happy for my sister. I couldn't do it Luna. I couldn't risk him getting custody of you two; I didn't want you having to go and visit your dad shacked up with your auntie. It was all too weird; I couldn't deal with it, so I left. I wanted a fresh start for all of us, and here we are."

I'm still trying to process all of this. "Did he have an affair because of me?"

Mum looks at me. "Luna, it was nothing to do with you, or Marley, or me for that matter, it was about him. He chose, he acted, he lives with the consequences; that's it."

"Why don't we see him?"

"He doesn't know where we are. Well, I suppose he could find out if he wanted to. I don't know why he hasn't, maybe it's his guilt or shame; I have no idea. I have nothing to do with any of them and I'm happy with that. If you want to get in touch with him, though, I'll help you."

I shake my head. I'm not really that bothered to be honest, not yet anyway. Maybe one day.

"I always said I'd never let you grow up like her though. I never wanted you to be spoilt, I mean look at Marley; Jeez, I over-compensated with him so much! I felt so bad because he was crying all the time; I just wanted him to be happy. So I gave and gave and gave and look at him now – pain in my arse."

We both laugh a little. "Shall we have a cuppa?" Mum asks as she gets up to make her way to the kitchen.

"Yeah," I say, thinking it's been a long time since I've just sat and had a cup of tea with my mum. Just before she leaves the room, I have one last thing I need to know.

"Mum," she stops at the doorway and looks at me. "Why didn't you tell me any of this before?" There is no hesitation, no dramatic pause, no time spent thinking of a suitable answer, Mum just says it; delivers three words that have the same impact on me as being hit in the face with a shovel.

"You never asked."

CHAPTER 18

I'm waiting for Sadie to say something now I've finished telling her about Mum's big revelation.

"How do you feel about it?" It's the first time I've been asked that question so I take a minute to think. I've talked to Mum about the facts, but not about how I feel. I don't really know any words. In the end I settle for an old favourite.

"Nothing."

"Nothing?" Sadie clarifies.

"Yeah, I don't really feel anything."

"Hmm... do you think it would be helpful to explore some of this today?" Sadie seems really concerned about my approach to the situation.

"OK." I'm interested as to where she could be going to go with this.

"How does nothing feel?" I give her no response, just sort of sit there staring blankly at her. Maybe subconsciously I'm trying to demonstrate 'nothing'. So I just sit there. Sadie reaches down into her bag and produces some pens, pencils, paper and a clipboard to lean on.

"Do you think you could draw it for me?"

I take some paper and a pencil, not because I think I have the answer – or any answer for that matter – but because I haven't drawn anything for ages. I used to love colouring in and all kinds of arty stuff, but I didn't take art or design for one of my subjects at school, so I don't really have the need to draw anything anymore and over time I have just stopped. Now with a pencil and paper in hand, looking like I'm ready to do something, I start moving the pencil. I am drawing the outline of an 'N'. I was going to write the word 'Nothing' in bubble letters but decide at the last minute that Sadie might think I am trying to be clever, so I let the pencil carry on and form a loop around the 'N' to disguise it. I need to get away from the now hopefully disfigured 'N' so I let the pencil shoot across the paper to the other side where I continue making loops and swirls across the page.

"I don't really know what nothing feels like. I don't know how I feel at all to tell the truth."

"It sounds like you're a bit confused about how you feel, Luna. Would that be a fair thing to say?"

I nod. "I don't know why I didn't ask Mum sooner. I don't know why I didn't remember the argument for all this time. I don't know why I've never really had any interest in my dad. Is that normal?"

"Luna if you find out what the actual definition of 'normal' is I'd love to know! It's what's normal to you that matters. You're not comparable to anyone else, none of us are. How do you feel about your dad now you know what happened?"

"Well I think he's an idiot, to be honest, and as for Auntie Alice, well I'm really angry with her, even though I don't actually know her. I don't know him either, I'm just angry with both of them which is hard when you don't know the people you're angry with. I can't actually do anything with the anger without talking to them and I don't want to talk to them so I'm stuck with it." I carry on swirling the pencil around the paper, not really thinking about what I'm doing.

"I feel bad for Mum. She's not a bad person, she's really annoying at times but I couldn't imagine her ever doing anything like that to anyone. I feel sorry for her. I think maybe that's partly why I've never really been bothered about wanting to meet my dad, because I thought he wouldn't want me in any case. And now I don't want to even if he wants to meet me because I'll never forgive him for what he did to Mum."

I look down at my paper. The pencil has continued round and round on the page as I've been talking, not really noticing that I was still drawing. I've been drawing circles, different sizes, some squiggly and wobbly lines but all circular in shape and all connected.

Sadie pulls her copy of my timeline from her bag. "I wonder, Luna, if this makes sense to you. Around this time you had the argument with Marley," she marks on the sheet just before the orange line. "I heard you say you weren't interested in your dad because you feared rejection from him?" I nod. "Look what happens next on your timeline." I look. It says 'Gigi moved away' followed closely by 'left school'. This is where it went red and the point at which I started 'not coping' with the anxiety.

"There were some very significant endings for you around that time; I wonder if there was a bit of a pattern-match that followed. You started feeling anxious when you had the argument with Marley. You coped with those feelings, then

121

right around here, Gigi moved away, and there was a big change coming in that you were starting a new school, so another ending with the old school and anxiety became too big to manage. I wonder if the feeling underlying the anxiety is rejection, or fear of rejection. What do you think?"

This makes a lot of sense. I have to think about it for a while, and I take a new piece of paper and start to draw again while I think.

"I think that's why I distance myself from people, like friends sometimes. They can't leave me if I'm not there to be left. I always expect them to think the worst of me."

"Have your friends ever said or done anything to make you think they don't want you hanging around?"

"Well, no. I just think they'd rather I wasn't there."

"So you base it on your opinion and not a fact?" I guess I do. I nod quite meekly, I feel like a bit of a fool. "Have you tried talking to your friends?"

"No, they wouldn't get it."

"What makes you so sure of that?"

"It's just what I think...." I stop drawing for a minute and look at Sadie who is looking back at me, smiling but with her eyebrows raised.

"Fact and opinion, Luna! Sometimes it might be worth stopping to think what it is that's making you decide something. Is it something you know, or something you think? Because anxiety can get in the way of making all sorts of sensible and rational decisions and it can convince you to believe things that just aren't true. It can stop you communicating. If you're not engaging with others and hiding yourself away, you're not communicating with others and it's a need that we all have that has to be met in some way. I wonder how things would change for you if you increased your communication by one conversation a day?"

"I'd probably do everybody's heads in."

"You don't do my head in, so again it's an opinion. The fact is, we communicate, you don't do my head in so you can't do everybody's heads in when you communicate with them." I kind of get what she's saying. It would be good to have normal conversations with friends, maybe I should try it.

In my head it's like a kitten has been playing with a ball of wool and it's got all jumbled and is now untangling, straightening out a bit. I am back to drawing circles and now both my pictures seem not too dissimilar from the ball of wool I have just described. It's easier to draw and talk and I've actually quite enjoyed it. I don't know why I don't draw anymore, I guess because there's no point. I say this to Sadie who tells me to 'do more of it'.

"I'm not good at it though."

"It's not about the end result though Luna, it's about the process of getting from a blank piece of paper to one that has something on it. It doesn't matter that you're not going to win any awards for it, you just said you enjoyed it and found it helpful, so do more of it. 'Sorting' is another good one to try, just to be in the moment sorting something, there doesn't have to be a point to it. You could sort a big box of coloured elastic bands or beads into their separate colours. It's about learning to sit in the 'here and now' and to be OK with it. When you try and think about nothing, you will probably think more, that's natural. Just acknowledge that you've had a thought and go back to what you are doing. Here, take this to get you started, I think you'll enjoy it."

Sadie hands me a little plastic bag with little bits of arty stuff in it. There are little beads, sequins, little wooden stick things, some googly eyes, all different shapes, sizes and colours.

"What do I do with it?"

"Sort them, for no reason at all. You can sort them into what they are, so sequins with sequins, or into colours or sizes, whatever you like. You could make something with them afterwards, a card or a picture. Just get some glue and stick them on. It's not a competition, there's no pressure. That's the important thing here, there's no pressure. When anxiety strikes you can spend hours and hours feeling like you're under pressure to do something or be somewhere, you feel like you've forgotten something, or you're worried about something – it's exhausting! Have a rest from it and do something with no pressure. You will have achieved something if you do it, so don't worry about how you could have spent that time instead, dedicate some time – ten minutes, half an hour, an hour, whatever you're happy with – but that time is to be spent doing a pointless activity, with no pressure."

I quite like the sound of that. I often find it easier to do things when I have permission and I'm actually looking forward to being arty again. I thank Sadie for the bag of stuff and notice that our session is due to finish soon. There is something I want to ask before it does.

"Sadie, do you think it's stupid that I got anxiety because my brother told me something that wasn't true and my friend moved away? Do you think that I should have been through something really traumatic to get it?"

"No, Luna, I don't think it's stupid. Anxiety is experienced by many different people for many different reasons. What defines a trauma? What makes something traumatic for one person and not for another? I don't want you to think about other people, I want you to think about yourself. Like I told you before, you're not comparable to anyone else; what you experienced was traumatic for you and that's what we're working with." I feel better hearing her say that.

"You're so clever," I tell her, spontaneously.

"Me? Why?" she asks.

"Well you worked out why I was anxious so quickly and now I'm starting to understand it all a bit more, you must know some really intelligent stuff to know all that about me, I bet you watched my body language and interpreted my drawing and stuff to know all of that didn't you?"

Sadie smiles at me. "Not quite Luna. You wrote it on your timeline."

CHAPTER 19

I'm lying in bed mentally preparing to speak to my friends today; 'communication' is the word of the day. OK, so let's talk facts and opinions. My opinion is that my friends will not understand that I have anxiety and they won't want to talk to me anymore because I'm too much hard work. Fact – I am probably hard work now anyway so nothing will change. Another fact – Gigi knows I have anxiety and she is still my friend. So I have one opinion counteracted by two facts, this makes me feel slightly better. I'm not sure if this is quite what Sadie meant by finding out the difference between fact and opinion but it's worked for now so I'll just do more of it; she will be so pleased with me! Today is going to be different so I'm going to try and make some small changes in my usual morning routine. Not quite sure what I can change but hey, I'm aware of it, this is going well. I feel quite good! Today anxiety can just do one.

I swing my legs out of my bed and sit on the edge. Instead of rolling out onto the floor as I usually do, today I decide it's a good day to rise with a little jump. So I stand up and do a sort of star jump. A little 'Woohoo!' accidentally slips out of my mouth as I jump, at which point I catch sight of myself in the mirror. Usually I would have recoiled in horror at the sight of the mad cow before me but today I find it quite amusing; so amusing, in fact, that I start to giggle. I go downstairs and look in the fridge. There's nothing good to eat as usual so I go back upstairs and continue my getting-ready routine. Wash, clean teeth, dress, tie hair up, pack bag, check bag, unpack bag, put everything back in bag, check bag, close bag, open bag, check bag, done. It's only when Mum shouts "I'm off now, Luna," up the stairs as she is leaving for work that I realise that either Mum is late or I am early. Mum's never late so I must be early.

"Bye then!" she calls. Now, I'm starting to notice already that this whole shake-up of my morning routine has been pretty rubbish and I have so far only changed it by doing a little jump as I got out of bed slightly earlier, so I need to shake it up a bit more. Usually I would shout 'Bye' back down the stairs, but today I am going to do it differently. I skip down the stairs to see Mum waiting by the front door for me to shout goodbye. I throw my arms around her, say "Bye, Mummy bear," and kiss her on the cheek. She looks like she's going to have a heart attack, not quite the reaction I was expecting.

"Are you alright, Luna?" she asks in hushed tones, her voice full of concern.

"Yeah I'm good, why?"

"You haven't called me 'Mummy bear' in years, just wondered if you wanted something..."

"No, I'm just shaking up my morning routine so I thought I'd come and say bye to you properly."

Mum hugs me. "It's nice to see you happy Lu....I will see you tonight won't I?" For God's sake this woman's impossible; she thinks I'm going to kill myself.

"Mum, I'm fine. I've been talking to Sadie about trying things differently, so I am, that's all."

"Ah Luna-Lu, I'm glad to hear it. I just want you to be happy, love."

"I know Mum. Can you let go of me now please?" Mum still has me in a tight embrace. She relaxes her arms and looks at me.

"I'm proud of you, Luna, I'm really proud."

"Thanks Mum." I hadn't realised until now how much it pleases me to know she is proud; how three words could change things. "Bye Mummy bear," I say one more time just as she's leaving the house. Today is going to be a good day.

I go back upstairs and get my bag. I *really* want to check it again, but I've already checked it three times; I know I have everything I need. It takes all of my willpower to not check it again before I go back downstairs to get my coat. Shaking things up a bit more, I grab a banana from the fruit bowl to eat on the journey. I manage two bites before I realise I would be eating in public so I throw the rest away, but not before congratulating myself for the fact I have actually eaten something. I put my headphones in and distract myself with my crazy imagination while I continue on my way to school.

At the gates I see Poppy and Amy sitting on the wall outside the new block. Before I have a chance to change my mind, I boldly walk up to them and say "Hi." They both look up at me.

"Hi," they reply in unison. "You OK?" Poppy asks. Shit. I haven't thought past this bit. My stomach starts churning, but not as badly as I expected, it must be those banana bites.

"Erm, I was wondering if I could speak to you at lunch time?" Poppy and Amy look at each other. I can't work out what they were thinking. I start breathing out, there's no point in me deciding what they are thinking, because I don't know and there's no time to ask as the bell has just gone. Before they reply, I tell them, "I'll meet you in the canteen at the start of lunch, can you tell Tara if you see her please?" and with that I walk off, no backward glance, no waiting around awkwardly for an answer, I say it and leave. I thought that went quite well.

The day passes incredibly slowly. If I wanted it to go slowly, of course it wouldn't, but today, I want it to be lunchtime so I can get this conversation over and done with, but instead every minute feels like an hour. I can't really concentrate in class; I keep playing out different scenarios in my head with different endings. It would start with me saying "Girls, thanks for coming, I'm really glad you're here. You might have noticed over the last few months that I've been acting slightly differently and this is what I need to talk to you about." In my head, I keep thinking if I had a real proper illness like cancer or a heart condition, I could tell them and they would probably be shocked and then cry, I'd have to pass them a tissue, they'd ask if there was anything they could do like donate a kidney or something, then we'd have a group hug and nothing I asked of them would ever be too much. I don't want to have cancer or a heart condition, that would be absolutely awful, but you get what I'm saying.

I'll tell them I have anxiety and they'll probably say "Well we all get nervous from time to time, Luna, what's your point?" Where would that leave me then? How can I explain it? I guess I could explain it like this: imagine if you're going into an exam. You get really nervous, your heart races, your palms sweat, and you feel sick; that's normal. That's a normal anxiety-provoking situation; you focus enough to sit the exam, you come out and think 'Phew! Glad that's over!' And everything goes back to normal. Now imagine feeling like you're going into an exam, with all of those side-effects, but there's no exam; there's no point when it just switches off, those feelings have become normal. Sometimes I know what I'm feeling anxious about, other times I just start feeling anxious about being anxious, just waiting for the situation to arise.

I don't know if they'll understand. I don't know if they will get that I don't seem to have an off switch for it. I'm working on it though, in my therapy. Should I even tell them about that though? Will they judge me even more and think I'm mad because I see a counsellor? Or will it help them understand that it's serious enough that I have to see someone? Would they get it more if I took medication? I just don't know. So I replay these scenarios over and over in my head until lunchtime. I go to the library at break so I don't bump into them, my plan is to talk at lunchtime and I don't want one of them seeing me and being accosted and forced to talk before I'm ready. I don't even consider this to have been one of my avoidance tactics, I am avoiding something which is necessary for me to avoid and therefore, it doesn't count.

As the clock starts approaching our one o'clock lunchtime, of course I want it to slow down a bit so I can spend a few more minutes in mental preparation. Does it slow down? Of course not; the last half hour feels like forty-five seconds. The bell goes and I wander over to the canteen. There's literally no one else in here and I start worrying that it's closed and no one has told me and now I'm going to look like an idiot. I take a breath and try to apply some logic. There's no sign on the door saying 'closed', the door isn't locked, there are kitchen staff working and I can smell food; of course it's open. Just as I come to my rational conclusion, a group of lads walks in and throw their bags on a table before walking over to the kitchen to get their lunch.

I've chosen a table by the window in the corner. I can see the door from where I'm sitting and my back is to the wall, so I know I've got no one behind me, which makes me feel a bit more comfortable. I still felt sick though. Time is ticking on and more and more people are coming into the canteen, more bags being thrown on tables, laughter, noise, shouting. I've been sitting here for about twenty minutes and they haven't come; I've been stood up. I take my phone from my bag and check the time. It's seven minutes past one so I must have been sat here for about four minutes, not twenty. Just as I'm about to give up, Tara and Poppy walk in. They see me and head over, both of them sitting opposite me.

"Hi," they both say in unison.

"Amy's just gone to the loo, she'll be here in a minute," Poppy tells me. Sure enough, Amy then walks through the door and comes and sits next to me, her face full of concern, which is unusual for Amy because she's normally the least sensible, or sensitive. I don't know how long it takes me to notice that they are all looking at me, waiting for me to speak. I try to remember my speech.

"Erm, thanks for coming..." This is going to be harder than I imagined. I feel like crying; why did I suggest this? All my earlier positivity seems to have left me when I needed it most. Story of my life.

"Luna, are you OK? Has something happened?" Poppy asks.

"I don't know where to start really..." I take a breath. I have nothing to lose – I must remember that, right now, I, Luna-Ray Jones, have nothing to lose. "I have anxiety. I've been going to see a counsellor for it, to try and help me. That's why I've maybe not been myself for quite a long time now."

The girls all look at each other. I'm sure this is when they are going to give each other an earlier rehearsed signal that basically means 'Run away from the mad one!' They don't. Instead, Amy was the first to speak.

"Is that all? Oh thank the Lord, Luna, I thought you were on drugs!" We all turn to look at Amy who has clearly given up on her sensitive, sensible side which has lasted all of about five minutes. I'm the first to laugh, closely followed by the other two. Poppy rolls her eyes at her and smiles.

"Amy! I can't believe you just said that."

"What?" Amy asks all wide eyes and innocence. "I did think it, I just didn't want to say anything. You even just said yourself Luna that you've been acting pretty weird, I didn't know what else it could be."

"So you're going to see someone?" Poppy asks.

I tell them what I can, about how it has been building up, that I had been referred to Sadie after I ran from class that day, and about how it has been making me feel. They listen. They ask questions from time to time and I can answer them because the questions are about me.

"Why didn't you talk to us?" Tara asks.

"Truthfully....I didn't think I could. I didn't really get it myself for a long time. I didn't know if you'd still even talk to me."

"I'm surprised I didn't work it out," Tara replies. All eyes switch to her to see what she says next. "My sister has anxiety. I guess I just didn't make a link, I didn't think you could get it at our age." Tara's sister is twelve years older than us and lives in a flat on her own, just outside of town. "To be honest, I've never really spoken to her about it either; I don't think she'd tell me anything anyway."

This surprises me, while Tara thought only older people could become anxious, I thought it would only be younger people. This is quite enlightening. Poppy turns the focus back to me.

"So what is it that we can do that would help you?"

"Help me?"

"Well yeah, I mean we're all kind of new to this, is there anything we can do that would help? Do you want to come out with us? Should we come to your house, or what?" Amy stands up. This must be the point where I have obviously become too much hard work and she wants nothing more to do with me.

"Who wants chips?" she asks. Tara and Amy nod and I just kind of sit there while Amy walks to the canteen to get the chips. I turn back to the two of them who are waiting for an answer.

"I don't know. I guess I didn't plan this far ahead, I thought you were going to say it would be easier to not be friends with me anymore."

"Why would we say that?" Tara asks.

"Yeah, that's really silly Luna; of course we still want to be your friend!"

"Why?" I ask.

"Well, I know things haven't been the same lately but we've always got on well. You have a really good taste in clothes and you're wicked at putting outfits together."

"Yeah and doing make-up," Tara adds

"And you can be really funny, some of the jokes we used to make up, remember the days we used to cry with laughter?"

"Don't forget the celeb spots, you were always the best at that, we don't play that anymore when you're not around," Amy adds as she returns to the table with two big bowls of chips.

I am stunned. I simply cannot believe they are saying all these good things about me. I guess I had just thought I sort of turned up to the party but didn't actually bring anything.

"Eat Luna!" Amy commands. I looked at the chips in front of me.

"I'm not hungry," I lie. The smell is wafting up towards me making me feel hungrier than ever, and as if to prove it, my stomach rumbles.

"As my old Granny used to say, Luna, if you don't put petrol in the car, you can't expect it to go!" I smile at Amy and her concern about me eating lunch. I don't like eating in front of people. I don't know why, it just makes me feel awkward. I might get food all over my face, or something stuck in my teeth and then I'll look silly. Or people would watch me eating and judge me. They'd be thinking 'look at her over there stuffing her face, greedy pig'.

I breathe out. OK, let me adjust this and add some logic. I'm in a canteen. It's lunchtime. Everyone is eating, including my friends and no one is watching them. If I get something on my face, I have a tissue in my pocket, I can wipe it off. I can go and check my teeth in the mirrors in the toilets before I go back to class. If I get something in my teeth, Amy would probably tell me anyway. I take a chip; it is really nice, so nice in fact that I take another one.

Poppy is talking about Luke Bailey. She still has the most enormous crush on him.

"I just need him to notice me," she is saying. "Hey Luna, do you still have an enormous make-up collection?" she asks. I half smile at the thought of my big bag of make-up – of course I do, I never throw anything away.

"Yeah I do as it happens, did you want to use it?"

"Could you show me how to do the liner on the top of my eyes, remember how you used to do it when you were an Emo?"

"Yeah, course I can."

"Wicked, come over to mine this Saturday and we'll get popcorn and watch films and you can show me how to do it." My smile fades. I am falling at the first hurdle.

"Erm..."

"Sorry, Luna, that was really insensitive of me, I just got carried away; would it be okay to come over to yours instead on Saturday? We can set a time limit or something if you want?" I feel bad now. She's trying; I have to do the same.

"No, come over Saturday. I'll get some popcorn and do your make-up and we'll watch films. It would just be easier for me to be at my house right now."

"Eeeek! Thanks Luna, Oooo I'm so excited!" She must have it really bad for Luke Bailey.

I smile as the others carry on talking. I feel really proud of myself. Not only have I made it through the awkward conversation, I've made a plan for Saturday and spent the whole of lunchtime chatting and eating chips with my friends.

CHAPTER 20

"So, how are you feeling about it?"

I've just told Sadie about Poppy coming over on Saturday. I have mixed emotions about it now; it's quite a big deal letting someone come into my safe haven. To everyone else it's a really normal thing to do – you have a friend over, you hang out, everyone has a good time and that's the end of it. The only person who has ever hung out with me in my room is Gigi. Letting someone else into my secret world is a big deal. I'm scared that Poppy will judge me. She'll see all of my collections and will probably think I'm crazy. Don't get me wrong, she was so supportive when I told her about my anxiety, all the girls were, but part of me worries that that was just to my face. Maybe behind my back they went off and had a good laugh about me. If I let her into my room, into my world, will she go and tell the others so they can all have a laugh at me?

The other part of me is looking forward to and actually quite excited about Poppy coming round, I'll actually have something to do. I want to be able to do normal things; I just wish it came more easily, without all these questions and scenarios racing through my head.

"I wonder, Luna, how do you feel about your collections?" Sadie asks me some random questions sometimes, I was talking about Poppy coming round and now she wants to talk about my collections.

"I don't get why you're asking me that."

"Well, I hear you saying that part of you is excited to see Poppy at the weekend, and another part of you isn't. I've also heard you say that you fear being judged about your belongings, your collections, and this seems to be the thing you keep going back to, it almost seems that the fear is around the collections and not actually about her being around you."

Interesting, I haven't looked at it like that before, but I suppose she might be right. I think about my piles of stuff.

"The thing is, I'm scared of throwing things away. I don't need all of the things at the moment but I get worried about what might happen if I don't have them."

"What's the worst thing that could happen if you threw your collections away?"

"Well... I might need them again."

"What is it that you have that you wouldn't be able to ever replace?" I think this through; I have to think of something. There must be something, just one thing. I think and think. I tilt my head to the right to see if anything drops from the left side of my brain and when that doesn't work I tilt my head to the left to see if that brings anything. I imagine my room – clothes, books, shoes, make-up, posters, old school books, old notebooks, old craft stuff that I don't use any more, posters, magazines, ornaments (well I say 'ornaments', I have a collection of plastic things that I won out of a 2p machine at an amusement arcade when I was much younger). I have to admit defeat here; I, Luna-Ray Jones, do not actually own anything irreplaceable. I answer Sadie's question.

"Nothing."

"Okay, so there's nothing irreplaceable that you might need, so what else keeps you hanging on to it?"

"I guess it makes me feel safe to keep it all."

"Hmm that's an interesting statement, 'it makes me feel safe to keep it'," Sadie repeats back at me. I don't respond, I know what's coming. "It's not making you feel very safe at the moment though is it? What you've been talking about so far is not feeling safe, it's quite the opposite. I wonder how you feel about perhaps sorting through your stuff and maybe parting with some of it."

I know what she's saying, I totally understand what she's saying, and she's right, she is right. So why does the thought of throwing things away give me a massive sick feeling?

"I'm not saying you have to go home and immediately dispose of everything, Luna, maybe just sort it through with the focus being that at some point in the near future, you will be letting go of some of it, even just one thing at a time. It's something to think about; I imagine your room being quite crowded with things, I wonder what it would be like to have some organisation around you? It does sound a bit overwhelming." Actually it probably is.

"I'm really worried about it though," I feel this is a good negotiation tactic.

"What worries you the most?"

"Well, needing something again."

"OK, so break it down a bit. Is there anywhere you could

store your things outside of your room – a shed, a garage, another room in the house – and then you can make a pact with yourself, that if you don't go and retrieve any of it after a month, it can go in the bin or be given to charity or whatever?" I think about our little shed in the back garden. I could put it in there I suppose, Mum wouldn't mind.

"Can I put one thing at a time out there?"

"Luna, you can do it however you want, whatever feels right and comfortable for you."

I feel motivated now, I can do this. I remember looking at photos Poppy has put on line before now of her in her bedroom, it's really lovely. It has baby pink walls, little fairy lights over the headboard of her bed, and it looks big and clean and open. I want my room to look like that. She will probably walk into my room and think it's an absolute shite hole.

We spend the rest of the session talking about me having the conversation with the girls, Sadie's really happy for me, she says. And it has actually led to having something to do at the weekend. I feel like my conversations are improving in general, I am practicing more. I might even speak to Marley. Well, one step at a time.

When I get home, I take everything out of my wardrobe. I have loads of clothes, most of which don't fit. So, although I have loads of clothes, I haven't really got anything to wear and spend most of my life in the same three outfits (on different days, of course). I make a pile of stuff that I know I will never wear again. I take a jumper downstairs with me. It used to be one of my favourites; it's a baby blue colour, knitted and quite chunky. I used to wrap myself up in it when it was cold and dark outside and it never failed to make me feel warm and cosy. I probably couldn't get my head through it now. I go downstairs and find Mum in the living room, lying on the sofa and reading a book.

"Mum, can I use the shed?" Mum looks up at me with a strange expression on her face.

"What do you mean use the shed?"

"Well, I want to sort my room out, I know it's time to let go of some of my stuff, but I want to have it near just in case I need it. Then if I don't need it within a month, I can throw it away." Mum can hardly contain her delight at the thought of my room being tidy.

"Of course you can, Lu, the key is hanging on the back of the kitchen door." I fetch the key and go outside, taking my jumper with me in a carrier bag. I leave the jumper in the shed, lock it back up and come back in the house.

"Mum, can I have my room decorated?"

"Decorated how?"

"Well, I'd quite like to have it painted, maybe get some new furniture, and make it a bit more grown up, a bit more me."

"Luna, you know the only reason you haven't had it done for years is because no one can get in it to do the work. It's a big job and there's so much stuff everywhere, it would be almost impossible to get in to paint. I tell you what, when it's tidy and you've got rid of some of your stuff, we'll decorate it together, how does that sound?"

"Brilliant! Thanks Mum!"

I skip back up the stairs and walk back into my room. I see all my belongings, quite literally everywhere. If I take away one item a day, I'll probably have my room decorated when I'm about twenty-two. I remember Sadie's words. "It's whatever feels right and comfortable for you." Now I have a big incentive, which kind of changes things. So I scoop up the rest of the clothes that I will never wear again and take them to their new home in the shed with my jumper.

CHAPTER 21

Poppy is due to come over in twenty minutes... if she comes. She said she was going to come. She might not come though. Maybe she will have had a better offer by now and she won't want to come any more. Maybe she never wanted to come over in the first place. She probably didn't want to come over in the first place actually but she was probably overcome with pity for me and just said she would. She will probably ring, but I won't answer anyway so she will leave a message and put on a really fake ill voice like I used to when I didn't want to go to school. She will tell me that she was suddenly taken ill overnight with a mysterious bug but all will be fine by Monday when she will return to school right as rain. Then I'll probably overhear her talking with Tara and Amy about going to town or something at the weekend and if I appear from out of nowhere they will quickly change the subject because they won't want me to know that she lied and then they'll start talking about how ill Poppy was and we will all say together that we really hope we never get ill like that. Then as soon as I'm gone again they'll all make a pact to always cover up for each other if they say they're coming over to my house because they won't really want to and...

"Luna, Poppy's here."

Mum's voice from downstairs snaps me out of my thoughts which apparently were kind of pointless because Poppy has in fact turned up.

"Just go on up Poppy, her room is at the top of the stairs." I hear Mum say this followed by the sound of Poppy running up the stairs. I go to my door to greet her.

"Hey Luna" she says as she comes into my room.

This is so awkward. I don't know what to say. I feel embarrassed by my room. It isn't a really awful room, it's a nice size but it is still quite cluttered. After I took my old clothes to the shed the other day, my clear-out kind of halted. I have started sorting my make-up out because I know Poppy wants me to do hers, so I have sorted through it so all of my good stuff is in one make-up bag, the rest of it is in a box beside my dressing table.

Poppy has taken it upon herself to go and sit on my bed as I stand awkwardly in my room, not really knowing what to do. I become aware of my breathing. Bubble breathing is coming so much more naturally now without having to actually blow bubbles, and I don't feel sick. Poppy has pulled a magazine from her bag and is flicking through it.

"Look I wanted to show you this," she says as she finds the page she is looking for. She holds it up to show me. I go and sit next to her and take it from her. It is a make-up tutorial, with instructions of how to create the perfect look, including the top lined eyes which I know is what poppy wants me to do for her. It looks really easy and I have most of the colours I need to create the look. I could blend some others if I need to, to achieve the correct shade.

"What do you think? I know it looks really hard, but I thought maybe you could give it a go on me?" she asks. It takes me a few seconds to process what she is saying. Is she making fun of me? Is she making excuses because she thinks I can't do make-up like this?

"Luna?" she says. I snap back into the moment.

"Sorry, yeah, I can do this no problem," I tell her.

"Can you really?"

"Well, yeah..." I am confused.

"Well, I thought we could do it later, I brought this with me as well, do you want to watch it?"

It's a chick flick that I have watched many times before with Gigi. I love it. It will be a good distraction for a while, while I get used to her being in my room. I put it on and while it loads I go downstairs and get us some drinks.

As we sit watching the film, both of us laughing in the same places as me and Gigi used to do, quoting the same lines – it is obvious she has watched this as many times as I have. I think about Gigi and feel a bit disloyal. I hope she won't be angry with me for having Poppy round and watching our film together.

We chat about who we like in the film, chat about other films, chat about who we thought was hot or not and so on. At first I thought maybe Poppy was playing the game, trying to distract my attention from feeling anxious, but when she says "Oh my God, you and Amy have the same horrid taste in men!" I realise that at some point, maybe she has had this conversation with Amy. Maybe this is just what hanging out should be about. And I, Luna-Ray Jones, am doing it. And it feels OK.

"Will you do my make-up then?" Poppy asks.

"Course," I say and get her to come and sit at my dressing table. I take my freshly prepared make-up bag and empty it out on the table in front of me. I have quite a bit of make-up, and this is less than a quarter of what's in the box that is now just at my feet. Mum buys me make-up quite a lot because she knows I like messing about with it, trying out different looks and taking photos of myself on my phone.

"Woah Luna, you've got loads!" Poppy states as she looks at the array of products before her. "I brought my own make-up with me in case you needed it, but it doesn't look like you do. I didn't think you'd have much to be honest."

"Why not?" I ask, feeling a little insulted.

"You never really wear it anymore. I know you did in year ten when you used to do eyeliner and mascara to be emo but now I never see you wearing it."

"I do wear make-up, just not at school" I tell her. I don't add that I only wear it here, on my own, for long enough to take photos of myself before it is wiped off, the only people ever seeing it being Mum and Marley, Marley not really counting because he probably never notices anyway.

I put a headband on her to keep her hair out of the way and Poppy cleanses her face in preparation while I get the colours, products and brushes together that I need.

I start with the foundation, carefully brushing it into her face bit by bit, before I get to work with the bronzer, using contouring techniques I've picked up to really give definition to her cheekbones and jawline. I make her promise not to look in the mirror until I am finished because I don't want her to see if I make any mistakes or question what I am doing because it will put me off.

I then make-up her eyes, using four colours all blended in, in different places to really bring the natural colour of her eyes out. I don't really need to do the liquid liner on the top, but it is what she asked for, so I apply it, almost expertly. A touch of liner underneath, just in the corners, again blending to a softer finish. Next I pencil in her eyebrows, they are naturally quite light and when Poppy does it herself, they end up being quite harsh and too big. I use a lighter brown than she would, which I think makes her look much more classy, although I would never say this to her. I finish off with a soft pink on her lips, a little gloss over the top. I am quite impressed! I need to just finish the contouring with a bit of highlighter at the top of her cheeks and along her jaw line, but I can't see it. It must be in the box. I flip the lid off with my foot and bend down to retrieve the highlighter which I can see is near the top. I must have left it there by mistake.

I finish Poppy's make-up and I'm really impressed with myself. What if she hates it though? I start to feel a bit nauseous at this thought and have to tell myself that it is only make-up, it isn't a tattoo or anything and if she really hates it, she can wipe it off and do her own make-up from now on.

"There, finished," I say, removing the headband and avoiding the strong temptation to wipe it off myself. Poppy turns to face the mirror and stares at her reflection.

"Oh...my...God..." she says, her voice low, with the kind of tone you might refer to as shock. She hates it. I brace myself for a barrage of abuse at ruining her lovely face.

"Luna, I love it! I can't believe you've just done this, I look amazing even if I do say so myself!"

If she's faking this, she's a pretty good actress. I think she genuinely likes it. I really want to be pleased with myself but I think if I do get a bit happy, something is bound to happen to take it away again. It is almost as though I am scared to be pleased with myself.

Poppy takes her phone out and snaps a picture of herself.

"I'm uploading this one straight away," she says as she adds it to Facebook.

"Do you really like it?" I ask, quite tentatively. I don't want to come across like I'm fishing for compliments, but I need reassurance.

"Luna, this is amazing, I can't believe you can do make-up like this, it's like art! Why don't you ever wear it yourself?"

I really don't know the answer to this one. I think I am worried that people will think I am above myself if I wear make-up, people will look at me, and I don't want to attract attention to myself.

Poppy continues to gaze into her own eyes, seemingly bewitched by her own appearance.

"Show me what you did," she orders.

I start to explain which colour goes with which brush and how to apply each product but Poppy has been distracted by something. Before I look down to confirm, I already know she is looking at the box by my feet. She nudges me away from where I am standing so she can reach it. She picks it up and takes it over to my bed, gobsmacked at the amount of stuff in there.

"Blimey Luna, you've got all this stuff as well!" she exclaims as she rifles her way through it.

"Yeah, the thing is some of that stuff is quite old" I say as she picks up a dried-out mascara and starts examining the wand. She opens an eyeshadow compact that used to have six colours in it, but now just contains a really ugly green that no one would ever wear. She looks puzzled as she continues to open things and it suddenly dawns on her that all is not as it seems. This is not an enormous make-up collection to be proud of. As she looks at it, it was like I was starting to see it through her eyes. It was a box of crap.

"Luna, why have you got all of this?" she asks.

I don't want to go through the ins and outs of my collections and my reasons for them, so I tell her what is fast becoming my truth. "I'm throwing it all away."

"Oh right," she says and as fast as she had picked the box up, she puts it down again and sits back at the dressing table so she can carry on looking in the mirror.

"Luna, will you do your make-up so you can show me how you did mine?" she asks. She seems really amazed by this. But then I suppose I have spent a lot more time practicing than most people would and I have got quite good at it.

I do as she asks, showing her the secrets behind contouring, applying eye shadow with all the proper brushes, the eyebrow tricks and Poppy looks on, hanging on to my every word.

When I have finished, she stares at me open-mouthed. "Luna, you look stunning."

I think she means it. Deep down, I know that I look good when I do myself up. I look alright without make-up too, but this is not something I would ever freely admit, even to myself. Maybe I should work on that.

"Wow, check this out!" Poppy says excitedly as she looks at her phone.

People have been liking her photo and making comments telling her how good she looks. Someone – who turns out to be Poppy's cousin who I don't know – has even asked if she has had her make-up professionally done! I am gobsmacked. Tara has seen it and written 'Did Luna do that?! OMG you look amazing!'

I would be stupid to think that I don't have somewhat of a talent here, but at the moment it is difficult to think that I do. I'm not used to stuff like this happening. Now we both have make-up on and both look pretty good, Poppy takes a photo of both of us together and uploads it, tagging me in it.

Poppy stays for dinner and I feel remarkably fine about eating pizza in front of her. We chat for a while longer, then it is time for her to head home. She lives about fifteen minutes from me and I offer to walk her halfway home. It will be some fresh air and exercise for the day.

Poppy says bye to my mum and we leave the house together, talking about random things. When we get to roundabout the half-way mark, and I prepare to turn round and walk back, Poppy hugs me and says "Thank you so much for today Luna, it's been great."

I hug her back and thank her for coming over.

"Luna I have something to ask you," she says which I anticipate will be the bit where everything goes wrong and something horrible happens. For this reason, I don't say anything, just look at her, waiting for her to speak.

"You know when we go to Prom, will you do all of our make-up please?"

"What do you mean 'all of our'?"

"Well, yours, mine, Tara's and Amy's," she explains.

"Well I'll do yours, but they might not want me to do theirs," I say.

"They do, Amy messaged me earlier, Tara messaged her

and suggested it and she asked me to ask you seeing as we were together today. I read the message when you went downstairs to get the pizza. I was nervous to ask you."

"Why were you nervous?" I ask.

"I don't want you to say no! Mum said she would pay for me to have my make-up done but I'd much rather you do it, and we have loads of time to practice it beforehand, if you want to of course."

I don't need to think this time. "Yeah, course I will!" I say.

There are a few reasons why I have agreed to this. One is because I have just sort of been invited to go to prom with them. The second, they need me for something, which feels good. And third, if we are going to meet to practice make-up between now and then, my spare time can be used doing something that I love, with friends. This thought makes me very happy. Almost as happy as getting home and seeing that since this afternoon when Poppy uploaded the photo of me and her, it has got seventy-six 'likes' and not one negative comment. It seems people are talking about me. And for once, I really don't mind.

CHAPTER 22

I feel I know Sadie well enough now to share something with her. I feel like this is my biggest secret; one I haven't told anyone until now, not even Gigi. It's a risk because she may now decide that I'm too much of a head-case for her to be able to work with, and that would be a shame because I have grown to feel comfortable with her. Comfortable enough to share this huge secret with her. I am filled with immediate regret.

"So what do you think it's about Luna?"

"What do you mean?"

"When you imagine yourself in these situations when you're a rock star or a celebrity or whatever, what do you think it's about?"

"I don't know. I'm mad, maybe?" Sadie laughs out loud and doesn't even try to contain herself.

"No Luna, you're not mad. I want you to think through this, though, and work it out yourself. We don't have many sessions left together so I want you to start thinking things through and coming to logical conclusions. And it's not that

155

you're mad."

"I don't know how to do that though."

"OK, let's break it down a bit. What's the common theme that runs through each of these scenarios you play in your mind?" I have to really think about this. I'm pretty annoyed with her for not just telling me the answer. Apparently there is an answer but she won't tell me what it is and that has irritated me somewhat. OK, think Luna. It's no good.

"I don't know."

"When do you find yourself doing this?"

"All the time."

"Are you doing it now?"

"No."

"So it's not all the time."

"Whenever I'm on my own."

"Do you do this all the time that you're on your own?"

"Well, no, actually sometimes I do it at school; I get in trouble for not paying attention because I've been daydreaming."

"So you don't do it all the time when you're on your own, and sometimes you do it when you're at school. Do you have a timetable that you follow where you fit it in?"

"Well, no, I just do it when I start to worry about something, it distracts me."

"There you are!" Well I never. I just worked something out, sort of by myself. "So when you're in these scenarios how are you feeling in the film that you're making?"

"I always feel good. Everyone loves me and I'm confident and I'm happy."

"There's one more word I'm expecting you to say...." Sadie looks at me in anticipation. I don't have a clue what she's waiting to hear. She registers this and asks one more question. "Are you ever in danger when you're thinking?"

"No, never."

"So if there's no danger then you must be..."

"...safe," I finish for her.

"Well done Luna, we got there! What you're creating in your mind is a safe place, which is exactly that, somewhere that you feel safe. For some people, a safe place could be a place they've known, a special bedroom they've had or a treehouse or a room in someone else's house, whatever. For some people it's a place they create themselves, up a mountain, on a beach, on a desert island wherever it may be. And it doesn't matter where that place is, as long as you feel confident and happy and safe. For you, it seems to be the thought of being in the limelight that makes you feel safe. It's easy for you to create a place where you have to think about doing something or performing or what have you, because you have a very active and creative mind. That's why we call this the 'safe place technique'."

"So I'm not mad?"

"No Luna, quite the opposite. You go to the safe place to stop feeling anxious. Over time the safe place might change but that doesn't matter as long as you keep the positive feelings. Go there every time you start to feel anxious or worried. Use the bubble breathing at the same time, or chewing or sucking something; that can be really helpful to feel calm as well."

"Chewing something?"

"Yeah, chewing gum or sucking on a lollypop or through a straw can help you feel calm. Try it! Next time you're eating or chewing, concentrate on it. Concentrate on how you're feeling when you're chewing and see what you notice about how you feel."

"I only ever feel anxious though."

"Really? Is that really true?"

"Well I only really notice when I'm feeling anxious."

"Exactly. So what if there are times when you're feeling calm? How would you know if you're not looking for it?" She might have a point. Thinking about it, when I'm away in my own head I don't feel anxious. That's why I like doing it so much. It's quite a relief to have told someone actually; secrets are such a burden. At least now I don't have to worry about anyone ever finding out that I do it because someone else knows now. To think I was already using an actual technique! I am quite proud of myself.

Sadie leans down and pulls something out of her bag. It is a small plastic tub with these little ball things in it. She hands it over to me and tells me to put my hand inside.

"What does it feel like to you?" It feels slimy. I pull my hand out straight away and look to see if there are traces of slime over my fingers. Surprisingly there aren't, there's nothing on my hand at all, it just feels wet. I put my hand in once more and the balls are definitely wet, not slimy.

"They're water beads Luna." I keep my hand in the pot gently picking up the beads between my fingers and dropping them back into the bowl. I took a handful and gave the rest of them back to Sadie. I don't look at how many I have taken, instead I close my eyes and allow the beads to fall from my right hand into my left, one at a time. They don't fall one at a time though because they are slippery. I try to guess how many are in my hand by counting the number I feel falling into my left hand – thirteen. I then drop them into my right hand and count twenty-two. I open my eyes so I can count them properly – there are nineteen. I'm surprised at how relaxing it is.

"I've got some here you can take home and grow." Sadie hands me a few small packets of tiny beads. "Just put them in water and they'll grow to this size," she says, lifting some of the ready-made ones from the pot. "It's important to relax, Luna. When you're in a high state of anxiety, your mind is on the go constantly. It's important to try and give it time to have a rest. You can use these, the breathing techniques, meditation – colouring in is really good too – whatever works for you. Try different things and see what you're comfortable with."

We spend the rest of the session playing with the water beads, practicing breathing and talking about school and life in general. It is at the end of the session that I decide there's something about Sadie. It's nothing bad, I know that, but I don't know what it is. It's probably me over-thinking things as usual; anxiety can do that to you sometimes.

CHAPTER 23

I think I might be making progress. Not loads, but just enough. I've been really good at doing all the things that Sadie has been telling me to do – I'm keeping my diary of food and sleep, I'm practicing my breathing every day. I haven't had any days off school; I've just been coming in and trying to get on with it.

The girls are being really good as well and we've had many conversations about make-up. I get the same kind of feeling from talking about something I know I'm good at and being asked actual advice about it, as I do from going to the 'safe places'. The biggest difference is that one is real life and the other isn't. As much as I love imagining all my lovely scenarios, they're not real. After talking to Sadie about it, I realised that I'd like to have those feelings of being good at something and being appreciated for something in real life and not just my imagination.

I've started helping out in the house a bit more too; a bit of washing-up and bathroom cleaning. Mum always notices and always says 'Thank you' and I like hearing that. I hate cleaning, let's not be mistaken about this, but I like actually having a job to do and seeing something go from being dirty to clean; it's satisfying. Until it gets in a mess again and I sometimes wonder what the point is, but I'll still do it.

I meet Tara just before we go into maths. I still really struggle with it. Miss Baker was the only teacher who didn't let me move in class. I'm still sitting in the same seat I was in on that life-changing day when I ran out. I think she might hate me more now because I swore at her. I was never made to apologise or anything, we have just never spoken about it.

I walk in with Tara. It's just after break and we are talking about prom dresses. Tara is absolutely terrified that she is going to turn up at prom wearing the same dress as someone else and they will be wearing it better. She's so gorgeous and has this really thick, lovely long hair that she is getting styled on the day, so I don't know what she's worried about. Even if someone is wearing the same dress, she'll still look beautiful. I haven't even thought about my dress yet – prom seems so far away, it hasn't actually made it onto my worry list yet. Just as we are sitting down, discussing ways to avoid the disaster that would be two people wearing the same dress, Miss Baker comes over.

"Is this something you want to share ladies?" she asks. Except she doesn't just ask us, of course she asks the question in her loudest voice so the whole class hears and the rest of the class turns and looks at us. I can feel my face starting to burn up. I don't like this, what's going on? Just earlier today I thought I was doing really well and now suddenly I'm back to feeling really sick again. I hate her. Tara isn't that bothered by her and just says with a straight face "No thanks Miss!"

At least she said something because I can't speak. I can't even move. I'm concentrating on my breath, sitting on my hands and pushing them hard onto the chair. I've discovered this helps sometimes too, just pushing down hard onto something and then letting my arms relax.

Miss Baker hands out worksheets. We are revising algebra. I hate algebra, I can't do it. In that moment I feel so useless. She's going to come over and make me feel stupid for not understanding. She's already made everybody look at me by having a go at me and Tara. I can't do this. I feel so shit because I thought I was doing so well, but I just want to cry. I can't stay in here.

I take my time-out card from my bag and leave it on my desk as I get up and walk out while I can still move. My legs are shaking – I hate this, I don't know where it has come from! I walk over to student services, which is where I'm supposed to go when I use my card.

I feel like I've got here quite quickly, but I can't really remember what happened on the way. I'm so frustrated with myself and I can barely hold the tears back.

As I walk into student services, Mr Davis sees me. His office is just outside and I walked past it as I came through the door. He comes to the door and calls me to his office.

"Luna, how are you?" he asks me. I still don't fully trust him.

"I left maths," I tell him.

"What happened?"

"I just couldn't stay in there. Miss started having a go at me and Tara for talking when the lesson hadn't even started yet and everybody looked at me and I know she hates me because of what happened before."

The words come out really quickly, anxiety seems to be affecting my ability to talk properly, and I'm not entirely sure he has understood what I am saying.

"Why do you think she hates you?"

"Because she had a go at us and the whole class heard! She wanted to embarrass me and it worked!"

Mr. Davis had a smirk on his face. He must hate me too.

"Luna, just think for a minute. Have you ever heard Miss Baker speak quietly?"

This has got to be a trick question. "Well no because if she was speaking quietly I wouldn't be able to hear her. She's never spoken quietly to me, she only ever shouts."

Mr Davis laughs. "Luna-Ray, the reason you have never heard Miss Baker talk quietly is because she never does. It's just her way, it's who she is, some people are naturally very quiet, some people are naturally very loud – Miss Baker is a naturally loud person. She's the same in the staff room; you can always hear her before you see her!"

I give this a moment's consideration. Now I'm really thinking about it, I guess he's right. She is just loud. She talks like that to everyone, but I only ever pay any attention when it's aimed at me. I think back over the conversation and Tara's response to her. Tara just said 'No thanks' to being asked if there was anything we wanted to share and Miss walked off. So what was I so worried about?

As Mr Davis is being so reasonable, I decide to tell him about how I think she hates me because of before and how she is the only one who didn't let me move or even ask me if I wanted to.

Mr Davis sits forward in his chair.

"Luna-Ray, I saw Miss Baker that day, she was actually

very worried and felt awful that you'd run out. She had no idea what was going on. I met with her that week when you stayed off and we had a long conversation about how to move forward with you. Miss Baker thought it would be best if she didn't move you in the class, because everyone in there saw what happened that day and she didn't want to draw any more attention to you. You've stayed in the same seat and you haven't mentioned it so we thought that was a good plan and that you were happy with that."

I'm trying to take all of this in. I feel bad now, so I just sit and say nothing. Mr Davis carries on.

"I think that maybe the fact we haven't mentioned what happened that lesson has backfired somewhat because there has been no resolution."

"What does that mean?"

"Well, we never drew a line under it. We didn't speak about it all together like we probably should have done, so the situation has never been resolved, as it were."

This is quite a good point.

"I can assure you Luna-Ray, Miss Baker does not hate you. I don't think she could ever hate anyone to be fair."

I bet she could. But I don't say this.

"Do you think it would be helpful to have that conversation now Luna – I know it was a few weeks ago, but if you think it would be helpful, we can arrange that?"

I shake my head. It's been helpful just talking to him about it. Not that I'm going to tell him this. I never even thought about Miss Baker just being the way she is. I genuinely believed she just hated me. It was like anxiety had put a cover over my ability to see the bigger picture. I sit and think about this for a while.

Mr Davis is looking at me. "Are you okay to go back to class?" He asks.

I nod. I go to leave the room and then I turn back.

"Thanks sir," I tell him.

I'm taking a slow walk back to maths and I'm going the long way round, to give me time to make sense of everything that has just happened. I had a wobble, that's all it was. I need to put it into perspective. Even a few weeks ago, I would have given up on everything at that moment, deciding that nothing was working, I wasn't good enough and what was the point in carrying on.

But it was one moment. One moment in the whole day. I'm doing my breathing as I walk.

I eventually make it to the classroom door. I muster every bit of strength I have and prepare to do one of the bravest things I have ever done. I know I have to do this. I open the classroom door and I walk back in.

CHAPTER 24

Goal-setting. I don't set any goals, I don't even think I *have* any goals and apparently this is something I need to work on. I told Sadie about what happened in maths this week and the fact I walked back in. She was really proud and then decided that goal-setting was needed this week.

"When do you feel you've achieved something?" Sadie asks me. When do I feel I've achieved something? That's easy.

"Never. I can't feel like I've achieved anything because I never do."

"You never achieve *anything?*" Sadie asks me, her voice going slightly higher in pitch at the end of her statement.

"Well, no." People achieve things all the time, I know that, they climb mountains and sail round the world and get A's in every subject they study, that's achieving things and none of those things apply to me so no, I don't achieve anything.

"If I asked you, Luna, if going to school each day this week was an achievement, what would you say?"

"No, it's not. I have to go to school."

"What about getting up and getting washed and dressed, is

that an achievement?"

"No, that's just something you have to do."

"What about coming here every session we've had, is that an achievement?" This woman is mad sometimes.

"No, I have to come here."

"What I'm hearing, Luna, is that your interpretation of achieving something is to do something out of the ordinary; something that is difficult. You don't see 'ordinary' things as being achievements."

"Yeah I suppose so."

"That must be difficult in itself; never feeling that you've achieved anything. Where do you get your feel-good factor from then?"

"I don't have one."

"How do you think life would change if you were able to feel good about things?"

"Well I guess I would be more positive, maybe."

"When you think of the 'ordinary' things, have you ever found them difficult? Have you ever found it difficult to go to school and stay in class?" I've already told her that I have, why is she asking me this? Oh wait... I know her well enough by now to know where she's going with this. I smile at her.

"You know what I'm going to say Luna! If things that people find difficult are achievements, then why isn't it an achievement that you've been in school and stayed in class all week?"

"There are hundreds of people in my school and they all manage it, so it can't be that hard."

"It might not be hard for them, but it's hard for you, and you've been managing to do it. You've achieved that. Getting up and dressed sometimes is difficult, it's a challenge when you're feeling low, but you achieve it... do you see what I'm saying?" Actually I do. I don't want to show it, but I'm feeling a bit proud of myself. I, Luna-Ray Jones, achieve things (sometimes).

"I wanted to look at goal-setting this week, I think right now this is just what we need." Sadie gets off her chair and kneels down on the floor rummaging in her bag for something. She produces a piece of paper and a felt tip pen. Then she produces some smaller paper rectangles and some cut-out hand shapes, all in different colours.

"Can you think of something that you'd like to be able to do, that you haven't managed to do yet?" I could be here for hours thinking of things I'd like to be able to do. I don't want to waste time thinking so I just shrug. "What about something in the community? A group you could join and feel a part of?"

I think of one of my favourite safe places, street dancing. I'd love to be able to street dance, but I can't actually dance; I can't move very well at all, my co-ordination is terrible. A few years ago, I'd gone with Mum to a dance event in the town and there were groups from all over the place who came on stage and show-cased what they did. I think that's where my original street dance idea came from. But that day, there was another class on stage and it looked quite fun. I was too young to join then, but I'd probably be old enough now.

"Zumba," I tell Sadie.

"OK," she says and before I have a chance to change my mind, she writes 'Zumba' in big letters at the top of the piece of paper. "Now this is the goal, to attend a zumba class." Already in my mind, I know this isn't going to happen. I like the idea of it and I wish I was brave enough but I just won't be able to go. Sadie pulls out some of the rectangular pieces of paper and hands them to me along with a pen.

"What is the first thing you think of that stops you from being able to go to a class?" Well there are hundreds of things that stop me, but the first that comes to mind is that I would be embarrassed. I tell Sadie this and she tells me to write it on one of the rectangles, which are going to represent my 'blocks'. "What do you think you would feel embarrassed about?"

"Well everyone there would know what they were doing and I probably wouldn't be able to keep up with them, so I'd look like an idiot."

"So we need a helping hand to counteract this then." Sadie points at the hands and I pick one up. "What would make it easier for you to go to a class and not feel embarrassed?"

"I could go to a beginners' class," I suggest.

"Excellent, write it on one of the hands." I do as she says thinking I've nailed this, but then she asks, "What else?" I can't think of anything else.

"Where would you stand in the class if you don't want everyone to look at you?"

"At the back," I tell her and take another hand to write it on there.

"Is there anything else you could do to make you feel more comfortable?" I think of Mum sitting outside waiting for me; I always feel better knowing she's there. Maybe she would want to come to the class too. I write 'Go with someone' on another hand. I don't want Sadie to know that I'm thinking of going with my Mum.

"Lovely, now stick all of these on to the piece of paper." I stick the block on at the bottom of the paper and surround it with the three hands. One problem, three solutions; if I'm not careful here, I'll be committing myself to leaving the house and going to a zumba class.

"What other blocks might you have?"

"Money. Classes are really expensive."

"Are they? How do you know?" OK so I've just made that last bit up. Money's always a problem as I don't have any, but I don't know how much classes cost, I've never looked into it before. I write 'Money' on a block and stick it above the block that says 'Embarrassed'.

"Get yourself a helping hand," Sadie tells me.

"I could find a cheap class," I suggest, proud that I've thought of it myself, and write it on a hand. "I could ask Mum to pay me to do some jobs," and I write 'Earn some money' on another hand, finishing off with 'Go once a fortnight' on a third hand.

Then I think of the biggest problem of all. I have nothing to wear. I write this on a block before I tell Sadie because I don't want her to tell me that this isn't a real problem. It is.

"Do you do PE at school, Luna?" she asks.

"Yeah, I have to," I answer.

"So you have a PE Kit you could wear?" I look at her in disgust; a PE kit?! Is she for real? I'm not even writing that on a hand, it's not even an idea up for discussion, we're not going there. Sadie laughs. "I can see you're not impressed by that Luna, but tell me, what do you think people wear to exercise classes?"

"Proper sports stuff."

"What's proper sports stuff?"

"Well proper sports tops and bottoms."

"Branded sports stuff you mean?"

"Yeah. I don't want to turn up looking like a tramp."

"What if you go a few times and decide it's not for you and you'd like to try something else? Sportswear, especially branded stuff is really expensive, Luna, and you don't need to have the full kit to go to a zumba class. Ultimately, what is it that people wear to exercise in?"

"Well, jogging bottoms or leggings and a t-shirt."

"Okay, so do you own some plain leggings and a t-shirt?"

"Yeah."

"So you're good to go then?"

"Well no, what if I turn up and I'm the only one wearing leggings and a t-shirt?"

"What if you're the only one that's wearing the full top to toe branded sports outfit?" Okay she's got me there. "You're planning on going with someone, right?" I nod. "So if both of you agree to wear leggings and a t-shirt, you won't be the only one there wearing that. If you enjoy it, and everyone is wearing the full sports get up, maybe you can invest in an outfit yourself if you're going to keep going."

She has a point. I decide my 'Nothing to wear' block probably doesn't have a place on my goal sheet, I'm just looking for problems, but Sadie tells me to stick it on regardless. I do so and counteract it with my helping hands. I look at the sheet.

"Can you think of any other blocks you might have?"

I honestly thought at the start of this little exercise that there were hundreds of things that stopped me from doing anything new, which is why I've never really thought about trying anything that I might actually enjoy. Things like Zumba classes are for people who are fit and confident and part of something, they aren't for people like me. I'm more than a bit disappointed to discover that my grand total of blocks is three.

"How do you feel now about joining a class?" Deep down I know that logically there's nothing stopping me, I just can't seem to suppress the voice of anxiety telling me I'll look a fool if I go. I explain this to Sadie.

"How many people do you think spend their good money to go to a class to laugh at someone else?"

"Probably none."

"Why do you think everyone else in that class has turned up then?"

"To do the class."

"How many of those people will know that you are going to be in the class that evening when you go?"

"Well, I don't know when I'm going myself yet, so none."

"And even if you do get some moves wrong or struggle to keep up, no one will probably even notice, because I hate to say it Luna, but lovely as you are, not all eyes will be on you."

I smile at her, I know she's right. Anxiety has this way of destroying all sense of logic and reason. I look at my goal-setting sheet; I thought I had hundreds of reasons for not doing things and actually when I look at it in black and white in front of me, I have to admit that I don't.

"Sometimes writing things down can be really helpful, Luna. If you write your worries and exhaust the list, you're likely to see that the number of actual worries is much less than you thought. When we're consumed by worry, it's easy to worry about the same thing in seven different ways. Then we think we have seven worries but we only really have one. Goal-setting is a really good way of managing worries because there's always a helping hand that you can put around a block.

You can apply this to anything you're finding a struggle. Sometimes you have to break things down as well, so instead of saying you're worried about school for instance, which part of it are you worried about? The journey? A certain class? Break times? Because when you break it down, you may realise that there are some bits you're OK with, so it's not all bad."

I get what she's saying and I think I'll be able to do this goal-setting on my own too. It makes a lot of sense. By the end of the session I have a whole new outlook on achievement. I *do* achieve things. There are things I find hard and I manage them and if someone else doesn't find it hard, then good for them, but if I find it hard and I manage it, then I've done well and I should be proud of myself. I'm really going to try and start thinking about this differently. Each night before I go to sleep, I'm going to write a list of things I have achieved in that day. Getting up, washed and dressed can go on that list. Going to school can go on there too. Even if I have a wobble and don't make it to a class, I can still say I went to school. I'm looking forward to this. I tell Sadie my plan and she really encourages me to do it. I feel happy; actually happy.

As I'm walking to the car with Mum, my goal sheet in my hand, I tell her about the session and joining a zumba class.

"Would you come with me, Mum?"

"Where is it?" she asks.

"Well I don't know yet, I'm going to look online tomorrow and see what's available."

"As long as you let me know where and when, sure I can take you and pick you up." She's not getting this.

"No Mum, I mean would you come to the class *with* me?

Would you come and do zumba with me?" We've just reached the car and Mum looks over the roof at me as she prepares to get in.

"You want me to come to a class with you?"

"Well, yeah... if you want to I mean..." I'm beginning to wish I hadn't asked. Mum's face breaks into a smile.

"I'd love to do zumba with you Luna," she tells me as we both get into the car. She starts the engine and begins to pull away. I can't help smiling to myself as she adds "But I don't know what I'm going to wear..."

CHAPTER 25

I've found an advert for a class on the internet. It's being held in a village hall and you can just turn up and pay on the night, you don't have to sign up for ten weeks in advance or anything. Mum gave the lady a call anyway just to check that it's okay to come along and she says it's fine.

We both agreed to wear leggings and t-shirts. I've found my outfit and got changed only to come downstairs and find Mum looking like she is ready to audition for a work-out DVD. I refuse to leave the house with her unless she removes the sweatband from around her head. She does, but I'm not sure she's altogether happy with it; she says her fringe will probably end up going frizzy. I have assured her that a frizzy fringe will be easier to live with than the emotional scarring her wearing a sweatband would leave me with. Why do old people not worry about other people laughing at them?

So we eventually leave the house and make our way to the hall, arriving early enough to make sure we can stake our claim on spaces at the back of the class. I start worrying that we could end up at the wrong end of the room if the instructor comes to lead the class from the other end, putting us at the front rather than the back. This is irrational though because I can already see that she has set up on the stage, her music system ready, her sports bag also on the stage, so it was clear which end Sinead, the instructor, would be delivering the class from. When I have settled this argument in my head, I have a chance to look around at who else is coming in. I thought I'd be the youngest person here, surrounded by old people, but that isn't the case. There was a real mixture of ages here, I can see a man – the only man – probably in his early forties but I'm not that good at guessing ages, stretching his legs to warm up. There is a girl a bit older than me and then a few other ladies between the ages of twenty and sixty. Not one person is wearing the full sports get-up. I'm so glad I turned up in leggings and a t-shirt.

As the clock approaches 7:30pm, the time we are due to start, the class members start to arrange themselves in four lines across the hall, and I am thankfully at the back. Mum and I stand in a line with another lady; I'm at the end.

Sinead welcomes everybody in and explains that we will work out in sections focusing on different areas of the body. If we need to stop we can, but we should try to keep gently moving, make sure we have enough space and don't get too close to anyone else and keep water close by.

The music starts and we have to move from side to side, shifting weight from one leg to the other; this is nice and easy, I can manage this. As the class progresses, so do the moves and even though this is a beginners class, it's starting to get a bit tricky. I find it difficult watching Sinead facing me and start to get a bit confused with my right and left. The lady in front of me has obviously done this before and looks quite good doing the workout, so I start copying her instead, which is much easier. The lady next to her however is not so graceful. Sinead shows the move, we do it, and then she takes it 'up-tempo' as she calls it, which basically means doing it faster. I watch the lady in front of me clearly getting confused and in the end she just starts doing her own thing. I really have to suppress the urge to giggle and this bothers me. Why do I want to do to someone else the very thing that had put me off wanting to come here? I was worried that people would laugh at me, but now here I am, wanting to laugh at someone else. Why do I do this? I think maybe I'm just nervous.

We have a five minute rest break before we do the cool-down, and the lady who's been doing her own thing comes over and speaks to me and Mum sitting on a bench drinking our water. She introduces herself as Val and asks Mum if it's the first time we've been here. Mum explains that it is and they have a conversation about how Mum is finding it. Val confesses to being a bit rubbish at keeping up with Sinead, but says it doesn't worry her because she's still doing something. She seems so lovely, I feel really guilty about my earlier urge to laugh at her. She even knows she isn't the greatest at it and actually doesn't care. More power to her I guess.

Mum's fringe thankfully hasn't gone frizzy which is a bonus because I would never hear the end of it if it had. The class is an hour in total and when it's over, I hear myself telling Sinead that I will 'see her next week' and I surprise myself in realising that actually, I am quite looking forward to it; I really did enjoy it. Mum did too and she wants to come again.

In the car on the way home I start wondering why I had made a big deal about going to a class. Why had I thought that people like me didn't go to things like that? All the other class members were just normal, everyday people, just like I am. I had noticed that Val was struggling to keep up a bit, but no one else had really paid any attention, as far as I could tell. I was focused on watching first Sinead then the other lady in front of me who seemed to know what she was doing. Nobody actually cared about what anyone else was doing, the one that was the most worried about it, was me.

What I did notice about tonight was that even though I was the youngest person there, I still fitted in. Val had come over to say hello but that was mainly to Mum and only to be polite. When it came to me, absolutely no one had even batted an eyelid.

CHAPTER 26

I don't know why I decided that today would be a good day to talk about my anger. I haven't really been feeling it lately, not so much anyway. There are times that I still feel the need to be annoyed but I think I'm getting better at dealing with it. Now, instead of just flipping out like I did before, I try the breathing, chewing gum or clenching my fists really tightly for ten seconds while I imagine all the anger I have coming into my hands so I can let go of it. The fist-clenching is reserved for when I am on my own though; I don't want to look like a twit.

"When was the last time you felt really uncontrollably angry, Luna?" Sadie asks me.

I pretend to think about my answer, but I already know what it is.

I can feel my cheeks burning as I say "When I told Miss Baker to fuck off before I ran out of school." Despite my feeling of shame, I accidentally let out a little giggle.

"I wonder if the giggle means you're a little nervous about talking this through, Luna?" I nod and try to think of something really sad in case I laugh again.

"So what had happened to make you do that?" I think back to that day which seems like five years ago now.

"I hadn't done some homework and she came over and had a go at me in front of everyone, I think I started crying and she told me to grow up. That was it."

"Was that really it? Nothing else happened that day?" I tell her how I had thought that Poppy, Tara and Amy were laughing at me in the canteen and that Tara had made up a story about Poppy and Luke Bailey, which it turned out hadn't been made up, but I hadn't known that at the time. Just before that was when Gigi had put the phone down on me to go and talk to Jay and I felt like I was getting left behind.

"It sounds like there was a bit of a feeling of rejection going on underneath it all – you felt rejected by Gigi because she went off to talk to her boyfriend, you felt rejected by your other friends because you thought they were laughing at you, your teacher then bawls you out in front of the class and tells you to 'grow up' which was the worst thing she could have said, because you felt like you were being left behind by all of your friends and it was almost like she confirmed that was what was happening by choosing those words at that time."

I reflect on this, it makes a lot of sense actually.

"Sometimes it feels like we can just 'snap', Luna, but I'm not sure that's always the case. Sometimes it's worth just sitting back and thinking of the trigger feelings. If we can make sense of those then that's the bit to work through before the volcano explodes."

"I don't know what you mean" I tell her truthfully.

"Anger is usually the explosion, but what is it that has

caused that? If you think about a good day — you're having a really good time and someone does or says something that annoys you but it hits your armour and bounces off because you have already decided that you're not going to let it affect you. Usually if there's a rage, there's something going on before that, that perhaps we don't acknowledge or pay much attention to, but this can be the trigger feeling. So if you were feeling very sad or frightened about something, you might not show this, what you show to other people is the anger. So you didn't tell your friends you were feeling hurt, rejected or fearful that you were being left behind, you showed anger. But it wasn't the anger that came first — does that make sense?" Actually it does now. "Are you using any coping strategies?"

I tell Sadie about the breathing and the clenching of my fists and now I sit and think about it, actually they are really helping. I don't feel as angry as I have done before, but I guess I'm also learning to manage my other emotions better too.

"How much do you laugh?" Sadie snaps me out of my little thinking trance with her bizarre question.

"A bit," I tell her.

"You know, laughing is really good for anxiety. Life is supposed to be fun and enjoyable, but sometimes we concentrate so much on the bad stuff that we forget we're supposed to be having a good time. When was the last time you found something really funny?" It was when I was on the phone to Gigi and we were pulling faces at each other but I'm not sure I should tell Sadie that bit so I just mention that Gigi made me really laugh a few weeks ago.

"A few weeks ago? That's ages! Do you think you could

try laughing every day?"

"Something funny might not happen every day."

"That's true, Luna, however it doesn't mean that you shouldn't laugh. You could find something funny on the internet or remember what it was that Gigi said and laugh at that again."

"It wouldn't be as funny on my own though."

"Laugh anyway. If I started laughing now, you would laugh too; think of it like yawning, you know when you see someone else yawning it's like you catch it and you start yawning too? Well laughing is the same. If you fake laugh for long enough, you will eventually start laughing."

I'm not convinced and Sadie must have known from my face because then she starts laughing. I think it's a fake laugh but within seconds she's laughing really hard. I sit and watch her, really wanting to prove her theory wrong, but the more I try to fight it the more I want to laugh at her laughing. I realise how nuts this must look and I fail to suppress a little giggle.

As soon as Sadie hears it, she points at me and lets out a squawk of a laugh and with that she has me. We sit there laughing so hard at absolutely nothing that tears are rolling down both of our faces. We compose ourselves and I take a tissue to wipe my face. We're both okay now and the point has been proved. I take a breath and compose myself, as does Sadie, and with that we are both off again. I have to admit, it feels good.

CHAPTER 27

I've been reflecting on how I come across to other people after that last session with Sadie. Sometimes I find something hilarious but I don't want anyone to know I find it ridiculously entertaining in case they don't think it is. It's like I want to avoid drawing any attention to myself so I have kind of lost a sense of me. Thanks, anxiety.

I've decided that I'm going to change this. Things have been going quite well for me actually. I've used my time-out card a total of seven times since I've had it which I think is quite a result. When I first got it, I thought that I'd be skipping out of each lesson at least three times, but I'm starting to feel a bit better in classes now. There are three reasons for this.

The first is that I've moved seats in practically every lesson so I'm always near the door and this has reduced my fear of puking in front of everyone.

The second is that I've started carrying an empty plastic bag from the supermarket around with me. I have worked out that if I have a safe puke point on me at all times, then I don't need to worry about it happening in front of anyone; I can discreetly use my bag and then just chuck it away. Sometimes, I'm a complete genius. Needless to say the number of times I have used my 'puke bag' is zero. But that isn't the point.

The third reason is that I have been handing all of my work in for feedback and I'm actually usually doing better than I had thought. There have been a couple of times when the teacher has said I'm not quite there but they've been able to see straight away where I'm going wrong and put me back on the right path. The end result is my grades are slightly better. Not massively, but a bit.

I also used goal-setting with Poppy, Tara and Amy in the canteen at lunch the other day – I don't always go to lunch with them, sometimes I'm still in the library, but if I feel like I want to have lunch with them then I do. And I actually eat and I do feel a bit better for having food inside me.

So we were all worried about revising because all we hear these days from teachers is about exams, like there's nothing else going on in the world, and we all started freaking out a bit. So I showed them Sadie's goal-setting task and we each did one around revision. We were able to share ideas of our helping hands as well and I'm now going to buy a bag of hard boiled fruit sweets that I can put between the pages of my text books. When I get to each page, I can have a treat – such a good idea! It was Tara's idea actually, although she is going to be using chocolate bars. I thought about doing the same but decided I would be too worried about having melted chocolate all over my text books so I thought to avoid this worry, I would go for the boiled sweet option. They were really impressed with goal-setting and I couldn't help but feel a bit proud that I had come up with something useful for everyone. Not that it was my idea, but if I wasn't anxious I wouldn't have gone to Sadie's and she wouldn't have been able to tell me about it and I wouldn't have been able to tell them, so basically, in a roundabout way, it was down to me.

It is the end of lunch and I am heading to my classroom to get there early (yes, get there early, I've realised that I feel better not being rushed along with the crowd so I make my way towards the end of breaks and lunch so I don't have to put myself through it), when I bump into Tara and Amy in the çorridor. Poppy has finally started going out with Luke Bailey which is wonderful news for her, but it means we don't see as much of her anymore. She hasn't ditched everyone completely, but it's just not unusual to sometimes come across Tara and Amy without her.

"Hey, Luna," they say in unison and I want to laugh so I do.

They both look at me in a strange way and I feel I had to justify myself so I quickly tell them "I just found that funny the way you both said that at the same time!" They both carry on just looking at me and I feel like a bit of a div. Now usually, this is exactly the kind of feeling that I would want to run away from, but today, it makes me want to giggle more. A brief image of me and Sadie laughing at nothing flashes into my mind, and I have to get rid of it quickly before I get the giggles.

"How are you both?" I ask them.

"A bit meh," Tara answers for both of them.

"We're both just in a bad mood today Luna, probably not very good company to be honest," Amy states.

"Has something happened?" I ask, my eyes darting

between their faces to see if it's something about me.

"Basically we've both just found out that our textiles coursework has to be handed in on Monday."

"Didn't you know before?" I want to know, concerned for both of them.

"Well, technically yes, but no we didn't," Tara answers. I give them the blank look and wait for one of them to elaborate.

"So the thing is, we were told the actual date apparently but we didn't hear it because we were talking, then Daisy Watt told us it was the month after it's actually due in. Smug cow."

I'm slightly confused. Why didn't they check with the teacher and then check again like I would have done? I guess one of the benefits of anxiety is that it inspires you to become informed. It is a known fact too that Daisy is the last person they should rely on for such important information, she can't stand them from what I can make out by the way they speak about her and how she speaks to them.

"So what are you going to do? Are you nearly finished?"

"Sort of...well no not really," Tara admits sheepishly.

"Me neither," confesses Amy. Well this is a turn-up. Maybe it's not just anxiety that stops you from doing work all the time, maybe it is just a 'thing' sometimes. They take it in turns to explain to me how they had to make a dress from scratch and write a load of stuff about it. I don't really get it, but what I do know is that they are both stuck on the actual making of their outfits and Miss Pattison has never really explained it to either of them in a way they'd understood. So they kind of carried on chatting for the best part of two years and are now on the verge of failure. These were my friends, I couldn't let this happen.

"Why don't you come round mine and ask my Mum, she'll help you."

Both of them turn to face me.

"Really? Would she?" They both ask.

"Yeah, my mum used to be a dressmaker, she has the mannequins and everything. She used to always try and get me to become interested in it but I never was. She'd probably love the chance to inspire somebody because it won't ever be me. Come round tonight after tea and bring all your stuff."

I am so excited to help, albeit via my mum, that the words are out before I've even thought about them. I've just invited them round my house, but actually, it's alright. I know Mum won't mind.

I lean back against the wall and my head knocks against something hard and I hear a snapping sound in my ear. I look behind me to discover I have leaned on a light switch. I flick it back off quickly, and then a thought crosses my mind. As I leant against it, no lights came on in the corridor. I flick it again. And off. On, off, on off. Tara and Amy are looking at me, both now more relaxed as they have an end to their worry in sight. I keep flicking the light switch as I look at them mischievously and say "Wouldn't it be funny if there was a teacher in the office and this was the light switch for it. They'd think they were sitting in some kind of rave," and I add to this effect by demonstrating some crap dance moves. It takes Tara and Amy a second to process what they are seeing, but then they start laughing. I start laughing. Poppy walks round the corner just in time to see two of her friends doubled over with uncontrollable giggles, while the third flicks a light switch on and off, waving her hands in the air like she's at a party, the sight of which makes Poppy laugh too.

CHAPTER 28

So many things have been going around my head. New things, old things; new things about the old things, old things about the new things. It's hard to describe.

I really want to talk to Marley but this would be an unusual event in itself. I don't know the best way to approach him. I know he's in; he is playing on his game station, I can hear him on it. I always know when he is on it because every now and then I hear an expletive when he has just lost, been shot or whatever. I don't even know what games he plays. I don't really know a lot about him any more to be honest.

I have a choice now. I can either sit and imagine what I might say to him (which will probably end up with me imagining a whole conversation and not actually having it), or I can just go and talk to him. Still unsure of what I am going to say, I get up from my bed and wander along the hall to his room. His door is slightly ajar but I knock on it anyway, to be polite.

"Yeah?" he says as he hears me knocking.

I walk into the room while simultaneously asking "Can I

come in?" as I sit down on his bed next to him.

"You're in now...what do you want?"

He never takes his eyes off the TV screen, his hands going nineteen to the dozen as he hits buttons, his breath quickening as he attempts to run from the opposition in what looks like a game about some kind of war. Whatever it is that he is trying to do, he fails and the TV screen is momentarily filled with a splattering of blood. It is quite grim.

He exhales loudly, clearly irritated by his game being over.

"You should try taking bubble breaths," I tell him wisely. "It will help you to feel calm."

"Whatever. What are you doing in here anyway?"

I am beginning to ask myself the same question; his room is disgusting. There are dirty cups and plates all over the floor, some still with remains of food stuck to them. The carpet seems to be his wash basket, dirty clothes strewn all over the place and I can see little bits of tobacco over the bedside unit which is obviously where he rolls his joints. The room has an old, musty smell to it, most likely due to the lack of ventilation in here; there is a window but it isn't opened. The room is dark and uninviting, his curtains still drawn despite it being the middle of the day. There is something about being in a room with no natural light that makes me feel quite weird. There's no natural light in Sadie's therapy room but that is different, there's no window in there. There *is* a window in here, but the outside world is blocked out which leaves the whole atmosphere with a depressing undertone.

I look at Marley, properly. I haven't looked at him properly for ages. He's lost weight. He has never been big anyway, he's always had a fast metabolism and can eat pretty much anything without ever gaining any weight. I am the complete opposite and only have to look at a slice of chocolate cake and a kilo will automatically attach itself to my thighs. There is something in his face that makes me think he has lost weight. His features have always been defined, he has always been good looking, but now instead of his jaw line looking chiselled and his eyes bright, his eyes seem to be sunken into his face and he looks, well, sad.

"What are you staring at me like that for?"

I didn't realise that I had been, but his words snap me back into the present. He still hasn't restarted a new game and is obviously waiting for me to say something.

"I just came to see how you are."

"Right. OK well I'm good, thanks for that, you can go now."

I don't move. I know why I came here and what I want to ask and I don't want to leave until I have my answer.

"Did you know about Dad and Auntie Alice?"

Marley restarts the game and breaks eye contact with me. "What are you on about?" he says.

"Mum told me. I just wondered if you knew?"

"Yeah I know."

"Do you ever think about him?"

"Not really."

"Would you want to see him if he ever asked?"

"Luna are you trying to do therapy on me?"

I laugh at this. "No, course not, I just wondered."

We are silent while he continues to play his game which appears to be based on violent death and general destruction.

"Do you have any racing games?"

We used to play two-player racing games all the time when

we were little. Sometimes Marley would let me win, I was rubbish at them. He used to be kind to me like that, he'd deliberately drive himself off the track so I could overtake and win while he was reset into the game. Then he would pretend to be really cross with himself when I beat him, but deep down I knew he was just giving me a chance. They were the good old fun days.

"Probably somewhere in there," he tells me as he points towards the cupboard his television set is sitting on top of. I slide myself off the bed trying not to get in his way while I root around the cupboard. These games are all so violent. Eventually I find it, the one we used to play. It looks so old and outdated now.

"Would this still work?" I ask him. As I hold it up, I accidentally cover the TV screen from his view, only momentarily, but long enough for him to run over a bomb that is detonated and kills him once again.

"Oops, sorry!"

He throws his controller onto the bed.

"Marley, why did you tell me Dad left because of me?"

His face twists up as he looks at me. "I never said that!" He sounds outraged.

"You did Marley, I remember it. You definitely did say that."

"When?"

"About three years ago."

"Luna, are you for real? I can't remember ten minutes ago never mind three years ago! Why are you thinking about that?"

"I was talking about it to Sadie."

"That's your counsellor isn't it?"

I nod.

"How's it going with her?"

"Alright I think. You did say it though Marley."

"Luna, I can't remember. If you say I did then I did, but I don't remember."

He doesn't remember. I believe him. I believe he doesn't remember, but I can't help but be a bit put out by this. I don't know what I would have achieved if he did remember, I don't know what I would have said, it wouldn't have changed anything, but he's not even denying it. We're not having an argument about it; I don't know what I expected.

He lifts the racing game towards me and says "Put it in then, let's see if this still works."

I do so and to our amazement, the game loads. The music comes on bringing with it a touch of nostalgia, stirring up fleeting memories from the hours we once spent playing on it. Marley hands me a control. We choose our characters and course and start to play. Some things never change and I am still totally useless at it. Marley isn't much better in the first couple of rounds to be fair but he soon gets the hang of it once again, but I don't.

We play and laugh, talking about the times we made bets about what the loser would have to do, reminisced of times we stayed up late, things we used to do, jokes we used to have. It is, dare I say it, actually quite fun. I haven't spent any time with Marley like this for years it seems. Somehow we have drifted from being brother and sister to two people who happen to live in the same house and have the same mother.

"Marley why do you smoke weed?"

"I don't." His tone has changed almost instantly, he is on the defensive.

"I know you do."

"Don't tell Mum." It seems funny that he would say that now, a grown man telling me not to tell mum, a request he regularly made as a child and we'd had a fight or he'd accidentally broken something.

"Mum knows," I inform him.

"No she doesn't."

"She does."

"How do you know she knows?"

"Because it was her that told me. You have tobacco on your bedside table and you smell of weed when you come in from being with your mates. It's not a big secret."

Marley has the decency to look embarrassed before he asks "Why are we having this conversation Luna? Are you getting round to asking me for a spliff?"

"Yuck no! Why would I want to smoke that?"

"Because it's the good stuff, Luna."

"No Marley, it's the illegal stuff and you shouldn't have it, it's not good for you."

Marley rolls his eyes at me. "Whatever."

Talk about a conversation killer. We've gone from happily playing our favourite childhood game, well my favourite childhood game, to sitting in an awkward silence. I don't want Marley to speak. I wish I hadn't brought the whole cannabis thing up with him. It isn't a nice thing to think about. He must have his reasons for doing whatever it is he's doing, I just feel sad for him. He looks sad, I feel sad. The whole situation is sad and I want to leave. We finish our round and I get up to go.

"It's been fun Marley, thanks for that."

I negotiate my way round the half of the kitchen that is

spread across his floor and make my way to his door. As I reach the handle, he calls me. I turn round to face him.

"Luna, I'm really sorry you know, for what I said to you, you know about Dad."

"It's OK Marley."

It is. It is OK. I feel better for him having said that. I know in that moment, there was something in his eyes, something in the way he spoke, something in his whole demeanour that told me what I needed to know, to validate me I suppose. He does remember.

CHAPTER 29

I've walked into the room with quite a sad feeling today. Sadie and I are now sitting looking at each other, neither of us saying anything. I think I might cry.

"So this is our last session together, Luna," I nod, not quite wanting to say anything in case the tears come and I look like a twit. "How are you feeling?"

"Sad...scared," I whisper.

"What are you scared about?"

"That this is the last time I'm coming, and what if I go back to how I was before?"

"What if you don't?" Sadie is gently smiling at me. I don't know if there is such a thing as gently smiling, but I felt like that's what she is doing. "It's an ending, Luna, and endings can often bring sad and scary emotions with them. But you have to have an ending to be able to have a new beginning. You came here because you wanted a new beginning, you wanted the anxiety to end, and here we are. You've worked so hard thorough this process and I feel that we're OK to end here and you can carry on doing the work on your own."

Sadie doesn't realise that the only reason I'm feeling better is because of her. If we stop now, it won't keep getting better; it will just stay the same. I tell her this.

"That's a lovely compliment Luna, but I really can't take the credit for how far you've come – you've done all the work. There are one hundred and sixty-eight hours in a week and we've spent less than one of those hours together each week. The process has actually happened in the one hundred and sixty-seven hours that you've been away from this room. I've given you suggestions and things to try; I've matched your commitment to each session when you have been in this room, but apart from that, if you feel better, then it's down to you." Now I really am going to cry.

"Was there anything you wanted to talk about today, specifically?" I shake my head. "Today we're going to do an overall review and if anything comes up we can talk through it. Is that OK with you?" I nod; head gestures seem to be about all I can manage.

Sadie reaches down into her bag and pulls out a sheet of paper.

"Remember this?" she asks, showing me a blank copy of the score sheet that I completed the first time I came here. I nod. "Let's go through this again."

Sadie asks me the questions which I couldn't really remember from the first time we did it. She asks me about sleep, eating, relationships, anxiety, anger and how I cope with problems, and I answer them all honestly. She then pulls my original form out and shows it to me as she says "Well look at that, you absolute star!"

The first sheet when I came was all scored at ones and twos. I remember thinking how crap my life was. Now I've scored all threes and fours out of a maximum of five. I smile; I am so proud of myself. I can really see now how much better I am, how much better I feel, but I wouldn't have known that without looking at the two sheets of paper before me, proving that my life is not as crap as it had been when I first came through the door. I feel like a different person – not the perfect person, not totally who I want to be, but better.

"I remember when I first came here, I thought you were a bit weird."

Sadie smiles at me. "Why was that?"

"Well you showed me the toilets, then got me water that I didn't want, then came back in pointing out things like the tissues and the bin; I thought it was a bit strange," I confess.

"Do you know why I did that?" Is she actually telling me she was being deliberately weird?

"No," I answer honestly.

"What was the biggest thing you felt when you came here for the first time?"

"I was really worried. And I felt really sick."

"I expected you to. You were referred to me as a client with anxiety, so I knew you were likely to have those feelings. I didn't want you sitting here worrying about being sick, because it's unlikely to happen. Anxiety isn't a bug or a virus, but the sick feeling is genuine. Subconsciously, you could have been more concerned about where to throw up instead of focusing on the session, so I showed you potential 'puke points' – the toilets and the bin. Then the worrying could have at least been confined to the thought of throwing up without the added stress and anxiety of where you could do it."

Maybe she isn't totally weird after all.

"I left the room to get the water so you could be in here for a minute or two on your own. Anxiety pressures you into knowing your surroundings, knowing you're safe, but wanting to do it in such a way that you're not being looked at or worried about being told off for not concentrating. So I didn't give you the choice of having some water in case you said 'no'. What would I have done then?! I could have made up a reason, but you might have known I was lying – how would you have felt then?"

"Probably more worried."

"Exactly! I just wanted you to have that time to have a good look around, to become familiar with your surroundings and for a genuine reason."

That was quite clever, I have to admit. I tell Sadie that she's right, I am always noticing things around me, it makes sense now why I do.

"So, let's look back, Luna. We've spent this time together looking at some quite basic things. Eating and sleeping were important issues; it's very difficult to work on anything emotional if your basic needs aren't being met, food and sleep being two of them. You've told me that both of those things have improved which is fantastic.

"We talked about anxiety and where it comes from, why it comes and I made it clear to you at the beginning that these anxious feelings will never go away completely, we wouldn't want them to, but what we did need to work on was managing those feelings. The first thing we looked at was breathing – bubble breaths – and the importance of the out breath being longer than the in breath. You have practiced and learned to be more in control of how you're breathing which in turn will help you to feel physically calmer. We explored panic attacks which are triggered by anxiety and again how to manage these. Remember the breathing is the most important thing, followed by finding another focus that will kick in the logical, thinking part of your brain, looking for five objects of the same colour for example."

I am nodding along as Sadie talks; already thinking I have learned a lot.

"We drew a timeline which enabled you to identify the time around when you began to feel anxious. Sometimes it can feel like you've always felt it, so that can be a really helpful way of reminding yourself that it came from somewhere and working around those trigger issues and feelings.

"We talked about the importance of communication; anxiety can stop you from talking to people and it's almost as if you have to practice having conversations again that are more than one or two-word questions or answers. Practicing talking to yourself can be a really helpful thing too, even in the mirror; we get so hung up on wondering what other people see, that we forget that actually, we don't see ourselves. We don't see our facial expressions when we speak to others, sometimes it can be helpful to learn what you do look like when you talk, because when you know, you don't have to wonder.

"We looked at 'fact' and 'opinion' and again how helpful it can be to differentiate between fact and opinion – how have you come to a conclusion about something? What is it based on?

"Goal-setting is a great task to help us be able to achieve things; sometimes we would like to do something but we don't try it without ever really knowing why. Goal-setting can help to break down those barriers, especially because it's in writing in front of you, it's not a load of stuff going round and round your head. Writing worries down can also be a big help; sometimes if we worry about something, we worry about that one thing in five different ways, so we think we have five worries. We don't, there's one worry that's been accidentally multiplied. A challenge I set for you was to start letting go of some of your things which you have been able to do and not only did this give you a sense of achievement, it literally created a space for you to be in that isn't overwhelming.

"You've enjoyed time with your friends socially and that's something you can continue to build on. You've also become part of the community by joining an exercise class with your Mum and now you spend time each week doing craft and drawing, just for fun.

"We looked at relaxation and finding a 'safe place' to go in your mind. You choose to be in a band or on stage where you feel super confident; that's fantastic, keep using it. You could find other places as time goes on, if you need to – on the beach, up a mountain, wherever – the feelings of confidence, happiness and safety are more important than the place you're in. Water beads are great too and you liked using them before, so do more of it!

"You've come a really long way Luna, you should be very proud of yourself."

I actually really am. Hearing Sadie talk back through it all is insane; it seems like I've been coming here for years, not weeks, we've done loads! I remember what she said earlier about me doing the work, and actually I have. I have done all the work, I've tried all the stuff out and it has been really helpful. I need to keep going, I know that. We talk through it all some more and reminisce a bit about my time in therapy.

"So what's next for you Luna?"

"Well I'm going to do my exams – they start next month – then it's the school prom, then after that I don't really know. I need to think of something I suppose. "

"How are you feeling about the exams?"

"Well, I'm trying to catch up, but I'll just see what happens. I think I will go to prom, Poppy, Tara and Amy are all going so I might do."

"That sounds good Luna; there's a lot to look forward to." We smile at each other again before Sadie tells me "Time's up."

We both stand up, we're face-to-face now. Before I know what I am doing, I throw my arms around Sadie and hug her. I don't usually like touching people or people touching me, maybe that's diminishing now too, who knows?

"I really, sincerely wish you all the best and every happiness, Luna. You're fabulous! It's been a real treat to be able to work with you."

Now I know I'm leaving, I feel brave enough to ask "Sadie, you know about anxiety don't you?"

"I've done a lot of training and a lot of research around it, yes."

"But you really know about it though don't you? I worked it out a few weeks ago. You've had it haven't you? Anxiety I mean, you've had anxiety."

I know and she knows that I know. It gives me hope. I know there is a way forward for me. If Sadie could find a way forward, then it is possible.

The last three words I hear Sadie say are "Yes, I have."

EPILOGUE

I'm looking round my room, everything packed in bags, ready to go, as I prepare to start my new adventure. I think back to when I collected my GCSE results a few weeks ago, imagining how I would have looked as I opened the envelope and saw that I'd totally smashed the exams and landed myself a much sought-after place at the best college in the country. I think of how I'd organised myself and packed all of these things ready to move out and live independently. Who would have thought? Probably not you, and you would be right, because that's not actually what happened.

I didn't get all the grades I would have liked to in my exams, but it's okay. I'm not leaving home to go to the best college in the country; I'm not leaving home at all actually. I'm staying here and I'm going to the local college who offered me a place on their Health and Social Care course. I've started at a lower level so I can re-take my Maths and English exams alongside it and I'm happy with that. So far, it's going really well. I prefer the environment to school, I like that I can wear my own clothes and I much prefer that I only have to concentrate on three subjects and not twenty (I know I didn't actually study twenty subjects at school, but that's what it felt like at times). I think I'm in a much better frame of mind now to fully concentrate on learning and revision. I missed a lot of school because I wasn't in many of my lessons. Even if I was there in body, I wasn't always there in mind because I was in such a high state of anxiety. I realise now what was happening. I still have some work to do on myself and that's fine, I'm in control and committed to 'me'.

I still practice the breathing techniques on a daily basis, I eat well, I sleep better, and I do more exercise. I've started meditating, which I'm not sure I've quite got the hang of because my mind still wanders, but I'm giving it a good go. I'm also thinking of joining a yoga class with a girl who I met at Zumba, Marie. She's really nice, a year older than me and we got talking because we were both pretty much the youngest in the Zumba class. She started coming on her own, she's so brave. Mum and I still go each week, well most weeks, and we both really enjoy it. Mum wasn't feeling up to doing the class last week, but she dropped me off and picked me up and I went in on my own. I nearly panicked about it but the faces there are familiar, Marie was there and the bottom line is that I went to do the exercise. I went to the class, I did it, I came home and that was it. That was the week that Marie and I got talking and she mentioned wanting to do yoga and asked if I was interested. She's new to the area and I think she's looking to make some new friends. Apart from adding it into my little book of achievements, which I still keep on a day-to-day basis, I like to be able to see things in front of me, to really be able to know and believe in them; it helps me out a lot.

I'm starting to recognise the difference in my feelings too; I know I was nervous about starting college, but I was also quite excited. It took a while for me to decide what I wanted to do, but I've settled on something; I'm going to work with the elderly. I like old people and I think being a Health Care assistant will give me the chance to be helpful which will give me a sense of achievement. Maybe after I've done this course and worked for a while, if I still want to, I could go into nursing. It's an option that I will keep open but I might decide to do something else and that's okay too. I did briefly think about doing beauty therapy, but I'm only really interested in the make-up side of it. There was a make-up course I could have done, but I want to keep that as a hobby, it's something that I enjoy and I wouldn't want to turn it into something else that could potentially take all the fun out of it.

As for my things being packed around me, I've packed them up so my room can be decorated. Mum and I are doing it this weekend; I finally finished sorting through my pointless collections! I do have some things left, I didn't go completely mad and chuck everything I own, but I now have just the things I need, with a few bits left over as keep-sakes. After I'd sorted my clothes and make-up, I began just letting go of a few things a week and I felt safer and safer each time I let go of something and nothing bad happened, so it just got easier. I got there in the end and now my prize is to have my room decorated. I've chosen a really lovely pastel kind of purple for the walls and I'm going to accessorize with some positive quote artwork. I've also got a big print of a butterfly that Mum got me a few weeks back. She said it's significant because that's what it's been like watching me over the past few months, like a butterfly emerging from a chrysalis or something. She's still very dramatic but we get on well. I think we've come to understand each other a lot better and having our Zumba time each week is something I really value now. I like that we can do something together.

I try and spend more time in the rest of the house or even out of the house now. I see Poppy, Tara and Amy and we've been to town a few times and out for something to eat and of course, I still do everyone's make-up. We did go to prom together and it was a really good night. There was a party afterwards at someone's house but I didn't go to that bit. The rest of them did, but Mum came and picked me up; I wasn't ready to go and spend time somewhere that was not very familiar, so I recognised how I was feeling and I acted on it in the way that was right for me.

I see the girls through new eyes now. Before, I was always so paranoid and over-thinking everything they said or did, and I missed a lot. I missed learning about them and who they are as people; I always thought Poppy was so confident but she's not as confident as I thought. She seeks approval a lot; she usually has to run things by us before she does anything. I mentioned it to her the other day when we were out and Tara looked at me and said "She's always done that though." I feel kind of sad about that because it makes me realise that anxiety stopped me noticing so much about not only myself but other people too. When I start to feel like that, I hear Sadie Rainbow in my ear reassuring me that it's okay for this stuff to have happened. Anxiety wasn't anyone's fault; it was just something that was there.

I know I make it sound like it's totally gone, but it hasn't. I know it won't ever totally go but I also know that it isn't supposed to. I'm really learning now to accept that there are things I can't control and I still have a specific worry time. I'm allowed fifteen minutes a day to worry but I never use all of it. It starts to bore me.

Gigi is of course still my best friend, and in October half term, I'll be going to Scotland to stay at her house. She asked me if I would come for the whole week, but my stomach churned at the thought of being away from home for so long, so we agreed that I would come for a long weekend – the Friday to the Monday – and I'm really looking forward to seeing her.

Marley is now on a waiting list to have therapy too. He knows he needs to address his smoking problem and I like to think that I have perhaps inspired him into giving it a go. Even he told me he has seen a change in me. We get on better now which is good, but a small part of me will always think he is a complete tool. I guess that's a sibling thing.

It's okay, everything is okay, and if it's not okay at any point, I know it will get better. I'm not stuck like I used to be. Sadie Rainbow once said to me on the way out of a session, that one day I might be able to use my experience to an advantage. I didn't believe her at the time but I thought about it and I decided that maybe my story would be able to help someone else. All I had to do was find a way to tell it. And I have.

ABOUT THE AUTHOR

As a young, single parent, Jess van der Hoech began her career by volunteering for her local Citizens Advice Bureau while attending night school to gain a diploma in Law. After gaining her qualification, Jess started her first paid role as an outreach adviser for CAB in the National Probation Service. This was where Jess's interest in the impact of trauma first began to develop. Jess went on to work and volunteer in Victim Support, supporting clients in the immediate aftermath of traumatic experience, quickly working her way through training, until she was supporting people who had been witness to or subjected to extreme violence and high risk and complex situations. Jess wanted to take this training further and after qualifying as a counsellor in 2014 she focused her continuing professional development on the impact of early trauma, fast becoming a specialist in this area. After discovering the need for a service in her local area that provided specialist trauma treatment therapy for children and young people, Jess founded 'The Gap (Bedfordshire) Limited'. *These Three Words* is Jess's first independent publication and her second book. It follows *What a Muddle* (ISBN 978-0995617803), a therapeutic workbook for children struggling with emotional regulation, which she co-wrote with Dr. Renée Marks in 2016.

Printed in Great Britain
by Amazon